A CUFF ABOVE

LEISURE ARTS, INC.
Little Rock, Arkansas

EDITORIAL STAFF
EDITOR-IN-CHIEF: Susan White Sullivan
KNIT AND CROCHET PUBLICATIONS
 DIRECTOR: Debra Nettles
SPECIAL PROJECTS DIRECTOR: Susan Frantz Wiles
SENIOR PREPRESS DIRECTOR: Mark Hawkins
ART PUBLICATIONS DIRECTOR: Rhonda Shelby
TECHNICAL WRITER: Cathy Hardy
TECHNICAL ASSOCIATES: Sarah J. Green and
 Lois J. Long
EDITORIAL WRITER: Susan McManus Johnson
SENIOR PUBLICATIONS DESIGNER: Dana Vaughn
SENIOR GRAPHIC ARTIST: Lora Puls
GRAPHIC ARTIST: Janie Wright
IMAGING TECHNICIANS: Brian Hall,
 Stephanie Johnson and Mark R. Potter
PHOTOGRAPHY DIRECTOR: Katherine Laughlin
CONTRIBUTING PHOTOGRAPHERS:
 Mark Mathews and Ken West
CONTRIBUTING PHOTO STYLISTS: Cora Brown
 and Christy Myers
PUBLISHING SYSTEMS ADMINISTRATOR:
 Becky Riddle
PUBLISHING SYSTEMS ASSISTANTS: Clint Hanson
 and John Rose

BUSINESS STAFF
VICE PRESIDENT AND CHIEF OPERATIONS
 OFFICER: Tom Siebenmorgen
DIRECTOR OF FINANCE AND
 ADMINISTRATION: Laticia Mull Dittrich
VICE PRESIDENT, SALES AND MARKETING:
 Pam Stebbins
NATIONAL ACCOUNTS DIRECTOR: Martha Adams
SALES AND SERVICES DIRECTOR: Margaret Reinold
INFORMATION TECHNOLOGY DIRECTOR:
 Hermine Linz
CONTROLLER: Francis Caple
VICE PRESIDENT, OPERATIONS: Jim Dittrich
COMPTROLLER, OPERATIONS: Rob Thieme
RETAIL CUSTOMER SERVICE MANAGER:
 Stan Raynor
PRINT PRODUCTION MANAGER: Fred F. Pruss

Library of Congress Catalog Number 2009931391
ISBN-13: 978-1-60140-987-4
ISBN-10: 1-60140-987-7

FOR EVERY DAY 6

Elizabeth Socks   8
Stacy Socks   12
Annelise Knee Socks   18
Emma Lace Socks   24
Iris Socks   28
Lucy Anklet Socks   32
Ivy Socks   38
Jenny Socks   42
Kristen Socks   48
Lacy Leg Warmers   54
Slipper Socks   57

CONTENTS

FOR BABY	60
Ribbed Cuff Socks	62
Lace Edge Socks	66
Ripple Cuff Socks	70

FOR THE HOLIDAYS	74
Nordic Stocking	76
Trees Stocking	80

GENERAL INSTRUCTIONS	84
YARN INFORMATION	94

{ A CUFF ABOVE }

One of my goals as a designer is to encourage, entice, and enable knitters to expand their range of techniques and explore the vast creative possibilities of the craft. I always hope that my patterns can provide a jumping off point for new adventures in knitting.

Socks are just about perfect for trying out new stitch patterns or techniques. If you long to knit an Aran sweater, but have never worked cables, a pair of socks gives you the chance to practice the technique without a huge investment in time or money (Annelise Knee Socks).

If your heart is set on knitting a lace shawl, but you aren't so sure about the prospect of working yarn overs, try out an eyelet or lace patterned sock to see just how satisfying this style of knitting can be (Emma, Lucy, Lace Edge Baby Socks, and Lacy Leg Warmers).

Slip stitch patterns offer a great introduction to color work, because you never have to carry more than one yarn in a round (Stacy). But color stranded work, aka "Fair Isle," is not as difficult as you may think (Ivy, Elizabeth, Iris, and Kristen).

Then there is the joy of wearing your own hand knitted socks or creating them for loved ones —these are such rewarding experiences! As anyone who has ever worn them can tell you, nothing is more comfortable than a pair of hand knitted socks. They are the best gifts you can give, and the nicest way to treat yourself to something very special.

With warm thoughts always,

Cynthia Guggemos

A VISIT WITH
CYNTHIA GUGGEMOS

When you love books, it's fun to work as an assistant in a library. And when you love to knit, what better profession to have than that of a knit designer? Cynthia Guggemos is happy to say her working hours consist of both pleasant occupations.

"I live with my husband and two cats in a small Wisconsin town," says Cynthia. "We're far enough away from the cities to enjoy the countryside, but I can still get to the bookstores. I'm also very lucky that my daughter's career allows her to live nearby right now and we can see her often."

When Cynthia isn't working, she still likes to be creative. "I like to garden, although I do it kind of haphazardly. I think you could call it 'cottage style' because it's casual. I put things wherever I would like to see them. It's that creative part of yard work I love, just like with knitting."

And what part of knitting has her attention these days?

"I am always fascinated by the variations that can be achieved with slip stitches. And I've seen a lot of Scandinavian influence on some of my designs. I've done a sweater in the Norwegian style, but mostly I love creating mittens and socks in that wonderful two-color technique.

"When it comes to yarn, I try to make it to fiber festivals whenever I can. It's very helpful to learn about the qualities of the latest fibers and see what's new in knitting. The Wisconsin Sheep and Wool Festival also has sheep shearing contests and sheepdog trials, so while I'm visiting the vendors, my husband watches the competitions." Cynthia pauses briefly to laugh. "It works out well for both of us!"

When Cynthia's knitting fans and friends want to see what she's working on, they visit her blog at www.baxterknits.blogspot.com. Cynthia updates the site regularly with photos of her knitting projects and her flower garden.

Cynthia says, "I hope that people will use my designs as a starting point for their own inspirations, changing their projects to suit them as they learn more about the art. Each time I start a project, it's a journey of discovery. I would like it to be that way for every knitter."

Editor's Note: It's no accident that Cynthia has authored this amazing collection of sock designs. She launched her design history with Leisure Arts with the highly successful title, I Can't Believe I'm Knitting Socks *(Item #4083, available at www.LeisureArts.com). As it became apparent how well these designs were received in the knitting community, Cynthia was commissioned to create the designs in* A Cuff Above. *We could not be more excited to bring you this lovely collection and know you will consider it an important addition to your knitting library. Visit us online to see all of Cynthia's designs which include* Lacy Baby Sets to Knit *(#4440),* Timeless Styles *(#4467), and* Lots of Love Knits for Kids *(#4659).*

FOR
EVERY DAY

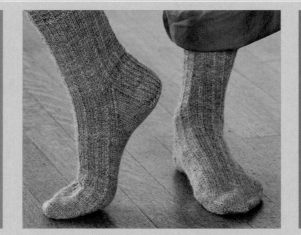

Up to the knees, mid-calf, or ankle-high—this collection of eleven sock patterns for adults has something for every comfort level. Your perfect pair of tootsie warmers may have cables or cuffs. The pattern may be lacy or twined with ivy. Perhaps you prefer Fair Isle, or a lighthearted pattern decked in boxes and dashes. You can also choose to forego the foot and knit a pair of leg warmers. Or go the other way to make cozy slippers. Most of these projects include a generous range of sizes. There's plenty of creativity here to keep you on your toes, with clear instructions that will help you put your best (soon to be sock-covered) foot forward!

ELIZABETH SOCKS

If you have never done stranded color work before, this is an easy pattern to start with. Only two out of ten rows involve carrying two colors, and the inserted Heel eliminates the need to work shaping in pattern.

 **INTERMEDIATE**

Finished Ankle Circumference:
7{8-9}"/18{20.5-23} cm

Size Note: Instructions are written for 7" circumference with 8" and 9" circumferences in braces { }. Instructions will be easier to read if you circle all the numbers pertaining to your size. If only one number is given, it applies to all sizes.

MATERIALS
Super Fine Weight Yarn
    [3.5 ounces, 437 yards
    (100 grams, 400 meters) per hank]:
      MC (Black) - 1 hank
      CC (Variegated) - 1 hank
    Note: If substituting yarn, allow approximately 220 to 240 yards (201 to 219 meters) of each color.
Crochet cotton thread or thin smooth waste yarn in a contrasting color - 2 yards (2 meters)
Set of 5 double pointed needles, size 2 (2.75 mm) **or** size needed for gauge
Two double pointed needles, size 0 (2 mm) for Heel
Split-ring marker
Tapestry needle

GAUGE: In Stockinette Stitch, in color pattern, 36 sts = 4" (10 cm)

CUFF
With MC, cast on 64{72-80} sts.

Divide sts onto 4 needles *(see Double Pointed Needles, page 88)*, placing 16{18-20} sts on each needle.

Place a split-ring marker around the first stitch to indicate the beginning of the round *(see Markers, page 88)*.

Work in K2, P2 ribbing for 1¹⁄₂" (4 cm).

Instructions continue on page 10.

LEG

Rnd 1: Knit around.

Rnds 2 thru 54{64-74}: Knit around following Rows 1-10 of Fair Isle Chart, 5{6-7} times *(see Fair Isle Knitting, page 92)*; then follow Rows 1-3 once **more**.

FAIR ISLE CHART

KEY

 - MC
□ - CC

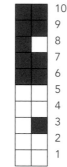

Follow chart from right to left and from bottom to top.

FOOT

The Heel stitches are temporarily placed on waste yarn. The waste yarn does not need to be fastened in any way, as it will be removed later to work the Heel. Leave long enough ends so that the stitches do not work loose as you continue with the Foot, allowing the ends to hang inside the Sock. When the Foot and Toe have been completed, the Heel will be worked by placing the stitches from the waste yarn onto two needles.

Note: The Heel placement is different for the two Socks in order that the "jog" in the pattern at the beginning of the rounds can be worn on the inside of the legs where it will be less obvious.

RIGHT SOCK ONLY

Rnd 1 (Heel placement): Drop the working yarns; using waste yarn, knit across the first and second needles, drop the waste yarn; return to the beginning of the first needle, pick up CC and knit across all 4 needles (Rnd 4 of the Chart).

LEFT SOCK ONLY

Rnd 1 (Heel placement): With CC, knit across the first two needles, drop working yarn; with waste yarn, knit across the third and fourth needles, drop the waste yarn; return to the beginning of the third needle and continuing with CC, knit across third and fourth needles (Rnd 4 of Chart).

BOTH SOCKS

Beginning with Rnd 5 of Chart, continue working in color pattern as established until Foot measures approximately $4\frac{1}{4}\{4\frac{3}{4}-5\frac{1}{2}\}$"/11{12-14} cm less than desired finished foot length *(see Sizing, page 86)*.

Hint: If you would like to check the foot length before working the Toe, you can work the Heel next. Just slip the stitches onto a piece of waste yarn first. You can try on the Sock and make any adjustments to the foot length; then work the Toe.

TOE

Cut CC and continue with MC only.

Rnd 1: Knit around.

Rnd 2 (Decrease rnd): K1, SSK *(Figs. 9a-c, page 90)*, knit across first needle; knit across second needle to last 3 sts, K2 tog *(Fig. 7, page 89)*, K1; on third needle K1, SSK, knit across; knit across fourth needle to last 3 sts, K2 tog, K1: 15{17-19} sts on each needle.

Rnds 3 thru 24{26-28}: Repeat Rnds 1 and 2, 11{12-13} times: 4{5-6} sts on each needle for a total of 16{20-24} sts.

Slip the sts from second needle onto first needle. Slip the sts from fourth needle onto third needle. There should be 8{10-12} sts on both needles.

Cut yarn leaving a 12" (30.5 cm) end. Thread tapestry needle with end and graft the remaining stitches together *(Figs. 14a & b, page 91)*.

HEEL

Lay the sock flat with the cast on edge towards you, and the waste yarn section facing upward. Place heel stitches on smaller size needles using either of the following two methods:

Method 1: Slide smaller size needle into the 32{36-40} sts immediately below the waste yarn sts. Slide a second smaller size needle through the 32{36-40} sts immediately above the waste yarn stitches. These needles will serve as holders. Pull out the row of waste yarn sts.

Method 2: Pull the waste yarn out as you slide the 32{36-40} free stitches at the front of the opening onto one needle, **and** the free stitches at the back of the opening onto another needle.

Note: When working the first round, correct the placement of any stitches turned the wrong way on the holders, by knitting into the back loop to avoid twisted stitches *(Fig. 4, page 89)*.

Rnd 1: Using larger size needles, MC and beginning with the holder closest to the cast on, knit 16{18-20} sts; with an empty needle, knit across the remaining 16{18-20} sts and pick up one st at the corner of the heel opening *(Fig. 13, page 91)*. With an empty needle, knit 16{18-20} sts. With an empty needle, knit remaining 16{18-20} sts and pick up one stitch at the corner of the heel opening. Place a marker to indicate the beginning of the round: 16{18-20} sts on first and third needles and 17{19-21} sts on second and fourth needles for a total of 66{74-82} sts.

Rnd 2: Knit across first needle; knit across second needle to last 2 sts, K2 tog tbl *(Fig. 8, page 90)*; knit across third needle; knit across fourth needle to last 2 sts, K2 tog tbl: 16{18-20} sts on each needle.

Rnds 3-5: Knit around.

Rnd 6 (Decrease rnd): K1, SSK, knit across first needle; knit across second needle to last 3 sts, K2 tog, K1; on third needle K1, SSK, knit across; knit across fourth needle to last 3 sts, K2 tog, K1: 15{17-19} sts on each needle.

Rnd 7: Knit around.

Rnds 8 thru 28{30-32}: Repeat Rnds 6 and 7, 10{11-12} times; then repeat Rnd 6 once **more**: 4{5-6} sts on each needle for a total of 16{20-24} sts.

Slip the sts from second needle onto first needle. Slip the sts from fourth needle onto third needle. There should be 8{10-12} sts on both needles.

Cut yarn leaving a 12" (30.5 cm) end. Thread tapestry needle with end and graft the remaining stitches together.

Repeat for second Sock.

STACY SOCKS

The Boxes & Dashes variation uses two related slip stitch color patterns on the leg. The Vertical Stripes variation, page 16, uses one. One pattern can be used alone for the entire length. Just remember to work a decrease round before beginning the pattern and an increase round after to accommodate the difference in gauge between the pattern stitches and Stockinette Stitch.
The Vertical Stripes variation, looks handsome in two solid colors, but using a self striping yarn for the contrast color really adds pizzazz.

 INTERMEDIATE

BOXES & DASHES

Finished Ankle Circumference:
7{8-9}"/18{20.5-23} cm

Size Note: Instructions are written for 7" circumference with 8" and 9" circumferences in braces { }. Instructions will be easier to read if you circle all the numbers pertaining to your size. If only one number is given, it applies to all sizes.

MATERIALS

Super Fine Weight Yarn **[SUPER FINE 1]**
[1.75 ounces, 166 yards (50 grams, 152 meters) per skein]:
MC (Grey) - 2 skeins
CC (Cream) - 1 skein
Set of 5 double pointed needles,
size 2 (2.75 mm) **or** size needed for gauge
Split-ring marker
Stitch holder
Tapestry needle

When instructed to **slip a stitch** (that is not part of an SSK decrease), slip as if to **purl** with yarn held to **wrong** side, unless otherwise indicated as on the Heel Flap. (On **right** side rows or rnds, the yarn will be held at the **back** of work and on **wrong** side rows, the yarn will be held at the **front** of work.) This will prevent twisted stitches and also prevent the working yarn from showing on the right side.

GAUGE: In Stockinette Stitch,
    32 sts and 44 rows = 4" (10 cm)
    in Boxes pattern,
    34 sts and 48 rows = 4" (10 cm)

Gauge Swatch: 4" (10 cm) square
With CC, cast on 34 sts.
Row 1: With CC, knit across.
Row 2: Purl across.
Row 3: With MC, K2, ★ slip 1, K3; repeat from ★ across.
Row 4: ★ P3, slip 1; repeat from ★ across to last 2 sts, P2.
Rows 5-48: Repeat Rows 1-4, 11 times.
Bind off all sts.

Instructions continue on page 14.

CUFF

With CC, cast on 56{64-72} sts.

Divide sts onto 4 needles *(see Double Pointed Needles, page 88)*, placing 14{16-18} sts on each needle.

Place a split-ring marker around the first stitch to indicate the beginning of the round *(see Markers, page 88)*.

Rnds 1-13: ★ K2, P2; repeat from ★ around.

Rnd 14: Knit around.

Note: When working M1 increase *(Figs. 6a & b, page 89)* between needles, place new stitch on same needle as last stitch made.

Rnd 15 (Increase rnd): ★ K7{8-9}, M1; repeat from ★ around: 16{18-20} sts on each needle for a total of 64{72-80} sts.

Rnds 16 and 17: Knit around.

Changing Colors: Carry unused yarn loosely up the inside of the Sock. Pick up the new color yarn from beneath the dropped yarn and keep the color which has just been worked to the left.

Rnds 18 and 19: With MC, ★ slip 1, K3; repeat from ★ around.

Rnds 20 and 21: With CC, knit around.

Rnds 22-35: Repeat Rnds 18-21, 3 times; then repeat Rnds 18 and 19 once **more** for Boxes pattern.

Rnds 36-38: With MC, knit around.

Rnd 39: With CC, ★ slip 1, K3; repeat from ★ around.

Rnd 40: With MC, knit around.

Rnds 41-43: Repeat Rnds 39 and 40 once, then repeat Rnd 39 once **more**.

Rnds 44-46: With MC, knit around.

Rnd 47: With CC, K2, slip 1, ★ K3, slip 1; repeat from ★ around to last st, K1.

Rnd 48: With MC, knit around.

Rnds 49-51: Repeat Rnds 47 and 48 once, then repeat Rnd 47 once **more**.

Rnds 52-67: Repeat Rnds 36-51 for Dashes pattern.

LEG

Cut CC and complete Sock with MC.

Rnd 1: Knit around.

Rnd 2 (Decrease rnd): ★ K6{7-8}, K2 tog *(Fig. 7, page 89)*; repeat from ★ around: 14{16-18} sts on each needle for total of 56{64-72} sts.

Knit every round until Sock measures approximately 6³/₄{7-7¹/₄}"/17{18-18.5} cm from cast on edge **or** to desired length to top of heel.

HEEL

Dividing Stitches: Remove marker. Using fourth needle, knit across first needle to last st, P1. The Heel Flap will be worked back and forth across these 28{32-36} sts.

Slip the remaining 28{32-36} sts onto a st holder for Instep to be worked later.

HEEL FLAP

Row 1: Slip 1 with yarn in **back**, purl across.

Row 2: Slip 1, ★ K1, slip 1; repeat from ★ across to last st, P1.

Rows 3 thru 26{30-34}: Repeat Rows 1 and 2, 12{14-16} times.

TURNING HEEL
Begin working short rows as follows:

Row 1: P 16{18-20}, P2 tog *(Fig. 12, page 91)*, P1, leave remaining 9{11-13} sts unworked; **turn.**

Row 2: Slip 1, K5, SSK *(Figs. 9a-c, page 90)*, K1, leave remaining 9{11-13} sts unworked; turn.

Row 3: Slip 1, P6, P2 tog, P1; turn.

Row 4: Slip 1, K7, SSK, K1; turn.

Row 5: Slip 1, P8, P2 tog, P1; turn.

Row 6: Slip 1, K9, SSK, K1; turn.

Row 7: Slip 1, P 10, P2 tog, P1; turn.

Row 8: Slip 1, K 11, SSK, K1; turn.

Row 9: Slip 1, P 12, P2 tog, P1; turn.

Row 10: Slip 1, K 13, SSK, K1; turn.

FIRST SIZE (7") ONLY
Row 11: Slip 1, P 14, P2 tog; turn.

Row 12: Slip 1, K 14, SSK; do **not** turn: 16 sts.

SECOND SIZE (8") ONLY
Row 11: Slip 1, P 14, P2 tog, P1; turn.

Row 12: Slip 1, K 15, SSK, K1; turn.

Row 13: Slip 1, P 16, P2 tog; turn.

Row 14: Slip 1, K 16, SSK; do **not** turn: 18 sts.

THIRD SIZE (9") ONLY
Row 11: Slip 1, P 14, P2 tog, P1; turn.

Row 12: Slip 1, K 15, SSK, K1; turn.

Row 13: Slip 1, P 16, P2 tog, P1; turn.

Row 14: Slip 1, K 17, SSK, K1; turn.

Row 15: Slip 1, P 18, P2 tog; turn.

Row 16: Slip 1, K 18, SSK; do **not** turn: 20 sts.

GUSSET
The remainder of the Sock is worked in rounds.

Slip the Instep sts from the st holder onto an empty needle.

FOUNDATION ROUND
With **right** side of Heel facing, continue with the working yarn and the needle that is holding the Heel sts and pick up 14{16-18} sts along the side of the Heel Flap and one st in the corner (where the Heel Flap meets the Instep) *(Fig. 13, page 91)*.

With an empty needle, knit the first 14{16-18} Instep sts.

With an empty needle, knit the remaining 14{16-18} Instep sts.

With an empty needle, pick up one st in the corner and 14{16-18} sts along the side of the Heel Flap, then knit the first 8{9-10} Heel sts; place a marker around the first st on the next needle to indicate the beginning of the round.

There should be 23{26-29} sts on first needle, 14{16-18} sts on each of second and third needles, and 23{26-29} sts on fourth needle for a total of 74{84-94} sts.

Instructions continue on page 16.

GUSSET DECREASES

Rnd 1: Knit around.

Rnd 2 (Decrease rnd): Knit across to last 3 sts on first needle, K2 tog, K1; knit across second and third needles; on fourth needle, K1, SSK, knit across: 22{25-28} sts on first and fourth needles.

Rnds 3 thru 18{20-22}: Repeat Rnds 1 and 2, 8{9-10} times: 14{16-18} sts on each needle.

FOOT

Knit every round until Foot measures approximately 2" (5 cm) less than desired finished foot length *(see Sizing, page 86)*.

TOE

Knit across first needle; move the beginning marker to first st on second needle. This is now the beginning of the round.

Rnd 1: Knit around.

Rnd 2 (Decrease rnd): K1, SSK, knit across first needle; knit across second needle to last 3 sts, K2 tog, K1; on third needle K1, SSK, knit across; knit across fourth needle to last 3 sts, K2 tog, K1: 13{15-17} sts on each needle.

Rnds 3 thru 20{22-24}: Repeat Rnds 1 and 2, 9{10-11} times: 4{5-6} sts on each needle for a total of 16{20-24} sts.

Slip the sts from second needle onto first needle. Slip the sts from fourth needle onto third needle.

Cut yarn leaving a 12" (30.5 cm) end. Thread tapestry needle with end and graft the remaining stitches together *(Figs. 14a & b, page 91)*.

Repeat for second Sock.

Finished Ankle Circumference:
7{8-9}"/18{20.5-23} cm

Size Note: Instructions are written for 7" circumference with 8" and 9" circumferences in braces { }. Instructions will be easier to read if you circle all the numbers pertaining to your size. If only one number is given, it applies to all sizes.

MATERIALS

Super Fine Weight Yarn
[1.76 ounces, 213 yards
(50 grams, 195 meters) per skein]:
MC (Blue) - 2{2-3} skeins
CC (Variegated) - 1 skein
Set of 5 double pointed needles,
size 2 (2.75 mm) **or** size needed for gauge
Split-ring marker
Stitch holder
Tapestry needle

When instructed to **slip a stitch** (that is not part of an SSK decrease), slip as if to **purl** with yarn held to **wrong** side, unless otherwise indicated on the Heel Flap. (On **right** side rows or rnds, the yarn will be held at the **back** of work and on **wrong** side rows, the yarn will be held at the **front** of work.) This will prevent twisted stitches and also prevent the working yarn from showing on the right side.

GAUGE: In Stockinette Stitch,
32 sts and 44 rows = 4" (10 cm)
in Vertical Stripe pattern,
40 sts and 48 rows = 4" (10 cm)

Gauge Swatch: 4" (10 cm)
With MC, cast on 40 sts.
Row 1: Knit across.
Row 2: Purl across.
Row 3: With CC, ★ K3, slip 1; repeat from ★ across.
Row 4: ★ Slip 1, P3; repeat from ★ across.
Row 5: With MC, K1, slip 1, ★ K3, slip 1; repeat from ★ across to last 2 sts, K2.
Row 6: P2, slip 1, ★ P3, slip 1; repeat from ★ across to last st, P1.
Rows 7-48: Repeat Rows 3-6, 10 times; then repeat Rows 3 and 4 once **more**.
Bind off all sts.

CUFF

With MC, cast on 56{64-72} sts.

Divide sts onto 4 needles (see Double Pointed Needles, page 88), placing 14{16-18} sts on each needle.

Place a split-ring marker around the first stitch to indicate the beginning of the round (see Markers, page 88).

Rnds 1-13: ★ K2, P2; repeat from ★ around.

Rnd 14: Knit around.

Note: When working M1 increase (Figs. 6a & b, page 89) between needles, place new stitch on same needle as last stitch made.

FIRST SIZE (7") ONLY - Rnd 15 (Increase rnd): ★ K3, M1, (K5, M1) 5 times; repeat from ★ once **more**: 17 sts on each needle for a total of 68 sts.

SECOND SIZE (8") ONLY - Rnd 15 (Increase rnd): ★ K4, M1; repeat from ★ around: 20 sts on each needle for a total of 80 sts.

THIRD SIZE (9") ONLY - Rnd 15 (Increase rnd): ★ K8, M1, (K4, M1) 7 times; repeat from ★ once **more**: 21 sts on first and third needles and 23 sts on second and fourth needles for a total of 88 sts.

ALL SIZES
Changing Colors: Carry unused yarn loosely up the inside of the Sock.

Rnds 16 and 17: With CC, ★ K3, slip 1; repeat from ★ around.

Rnds 18 and 19: With MC, K1, slip 1, ★ K3, slip 1; repeat from ★ around to last 2 sts, K2.

Repeat Rnds 16-19 for Vertical Stripe pattern until Cuff measures approximately 5¼{5½-5¾}"/ 13.5{14-14.5} cm from cast on edge **or** 1½" (4 cm) less than desired length to top of heel, ending by working Rnd 19.

LEG
Cut CC and complete Sock with MC.

Next Rnd: Knit around.

FIRST SIZE (7") ONLY - Decrease Rnd: ★ K2, K2 tog (Fig. 7, page 89), (K4, K2 tog) 5 times; repeat from ★ once **more**: 14 sts on each needle for a total of 56 sts.

SECOND SIZE (8") ONLY - Decrease Rnd: ★ K3, K2 tog (Fig. 7, page 89); repeat from ★ around: 16 sts on each needle for a total of 64 sts.

THIRD SIZE (9") ONLY - Decrease Rnd: ★ K7, K2 tog (Fig. 7, page 89), (K3, K2 tog) 7 times; repeat from ★ once **more**: 18 sts on each needle for a total of 72 sts.

Knit every round until Sock measures approximately 6¾{7-7¼}"/17{18-18.5} cm from cast on edge **or** to desired length to top of heel.

Beginning with Heel, complete same as Stacy Boxes & Dashes, page 14.

Repeat for second Sock.

ANNELISE KNEE SOCKS

Knee socks are great for fashion with the added benefit of keeping your legs warm. These have shaping for a perfect fit. Chose from Ladder Cables, page 22, and Crossed Cables.

{ CROSSED CABLES }

Finished Calf Circumference:
12¼{13¾-15½}"/31{35-39.5} cm

Size Note: The Cable Panels have a lot of stretch. For a good fit, choose your size based on a calf circumference of up to 1½" to 2" (4 to 5 cm) less than your actual calf measurement.
Instructions are written for 12¼" circumference with 13¾" and 15½" circumference in braces { }. Instructions will be easier to read if you circle all the numbers pertaining to your size. If only one number is given, it applies to all sizes.

MATERIALS
Medium Weight Yarn
   [3 ounces, 197 yards
   (85 grams, 180 meters) per skein]:
     2{3-3} skeins
Set of 5 double pointed needles,
   size 7 (4.5 mm) **or** size needed for gauge
Cable needle
Split-ring markers - 3
Stitch holder
Yarn needle

GAUGE: In Stockinette Stitch,
   20 sts and 26 rows = 4" (10 cm)
   Cable panel, 17 sts = 2½" (6.25 cm)
   unblocked

Instructions continue on page 20.

STITCH GUIDE

BACK CABLE (uses 4 sts)
Slip next 2 sts onto cable needle and hold in **back** of work, K2 from left needle, K2 from cable needle.

FRONT CABLE (uses 4 sts)
Slip next 2 sts onto cable needle and hold in **front** of work, K2 from left needle, K2 from cable needle.

RIGHT TWIST (uses 2 sts)
K2 tog but do **not** slip sts off needle *(Fig. 1a)*, then knit the first st letting both sts drop off the needle *(Fig. 1b)*.

Fig. 1a	**Fig. 1b**
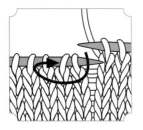	

LEFT TWIST (uses 2 sts)
Knit into the back loop of second st on left needle but do **not** slip sts off needle *(Fig. 2)*, then knit first 2 sts together through back loop *(Fig. 4, page 89)*, letting both sts drop off the needle.

Fig. 2

CABLE PANEL (uses 17 sts)
Row 1: K1, P1, Right Twist, P1, Front Cable, K3, P1, Left Twist, P1, K1.
Row 2: K1, P1, K2, P1, K7, P1, K2, P1, K1.
Row 3: K1, P1, Right Twist, P1, K3, Back Cable, P1, Left Twist, P1, K1.
Row 4: K1, P1, K2, P1, K7, P1, K2, P1, K1.
Repeat Rows 1-4 for Cable Panel.

CUFF

Cast on 68{76-84} sts.

Divide sts onto 4 needles *(see **Double Pointed Needles**, page 88)*, placing 17{19-21} sts on each needle.

Place a split-ring marker around the first stitch to indicate the beginning of the round *(see **Markers**, page 88)*.

Work in K1, P1 ribbing for 1½" (4 cm).

LEG

Rearrange the sts, slipping 1{3-5} st(s) from first needle onto second needle and 1{3-5} st(s) from third needle onto fourth needle: 16 sts on first and third needles and 18{22-26} sts on second and fourth needles.

Increase Rnd: ★ K1, P1, K2, P1, K3, M1 *(Figs. 6a & b, page 89)*, K3, P1, K2, P1, K1, knit across next needle; repeat from ★ once **more**: 17 sts on first and third needles for a total of 70{78-86} sts.

Rnd 1: Work Cable Panel, knit across second needle, work Cable Panel, knit across.

Repeat Rnd 1 for pattern until Sock measures approximately 4" (10 cm) from cast on edge.

Decrease Rnd: ★ Work Cable Panel, K2 tog *(Fig. 7, page 89)*, knit across to last 2 sts on same needle, SSK *(Figs. 9a-c, page 90)*; repeat from ★ once **more**: 66{74-82} sts.

Continuing in established pattern, repeat decrease round every eighth round, 5{6-7} times: 6{8-10} sts on second and fourth needle for a total of 46{50-54} sts.

Work even until Sock measures approximately 13{13¾-14½}"/33{35-37} cm from cast on edge **or** desired length to top of heel, ending by working Row 1 of Cable panel.

HEEL

Dividing Stitches: Slip last 1{2-3} st(s) from fourth needle onto empty needle, remove marker, continuing with same needle, knit across first needle and 1{2-3} st(s) from second needle. The Heel Flap will be worked back and forth across these 19{21-23} sts.

Slip remaining 27{29-31} sts onto a st holder for Instep to be worked later.

HEEL FLAP

When instructed to **slip a stitch** while working the Heel (that is not part of an SSK decrease), slip as if to **purl** with yarn held to **wrong** side. (On **right** side rows, the yarn will be held at the **back** of work and on **wrong** side rows, the yarn will be held at the **front** of work.) This will prevent twisted stitches and also prevent the working yarn from showing on the right side.

Row 1: Purl across.

Row 2: Slip 1, ★ K1, slip 1; repeat from ★ across.

Rows 3 thru 18{20-22}: Repeat Rows 1 and 2, 8{9-10} times.

TURNING HEEL

Begin working short rows as follows:

Row 1: P 12{13-14}, P2 tog *(Fig. 12, page 91)*, P1, leave remaining 4{5-6} sts unworked; **turn**.

Row 2: Slip 1, K6, SSK, K1, leave remaining 4{5-6} sts unworked; turn.

Row 3: Slip 1, P7, P2 tog, P1; turn.

Row 4: Slip 1, K8, SSK, K1; turn.

Row 5: Slip 1, P9, P2 tog, P1; turn.

FIRST SIZE (12¼") ONLY
Row 6: Slip 1, K 10, SSK, K1; do **not** turn: 13 sts.

SECOND SIZE (13¾") ONLY
Row 6: Slip 1, K 10, SSK, K1; turn.

Row 7: Slip 1, P 11, P2 tog; turn.

Row 8: Slip 1, K 11, SSK; do **not** turn: 13 sts.

THIRD SIZE (15½") ONLY
Row 6: Slip 1, K 10, SSK, K1; turn.

Row 7: Slip 1, P 11, P2 tog, P1; turn.

Row 8: Slip 1, K 12, SSK, K1; do **not** turn: 15 sts.

GUSSET

The remainder of the Sock is worked in rounds on 3 needles.

Slip the Instep sts from the st holder onto an empty needle.

FOUNDATION ROUND

With **right** side of Heel facing, continue with the working yarn and the needle that is holding the Heel sts and pick up 9{10-11} sts along the side of the Heel Flap and one st in the corner (where the Heel Flap meets the Instep) *(Fig. 13, page 91)*, K1 from Instep needle.

With an empty needle and working across Instep sts, K4{5-6}, place marker, work Row 2 of Cable Panel, place marker, knit across to last st.

With an empty needle, K1 from Instep needle, pick up one st in the corner and 9{10-11} sts along the side of the Heel Flap, then knit the first 6{6-7} Heel sts; place a marker around the first st on the next needle to indicate the beginning of the round.

There should be 18{19-21} sts on first needle, 25{27-29} sts on second needle, and 17{18-20} sts on third needle for a total of 60{64-70} sts.

GUSSET DECREASES

Rnd 1: Work around.

Rnd 2 (Decrease rnd): Knit across to last 3 sts on first needle, K2 tog, K1; work across second needle; on third needle K1, SSK, knit across: 17{18-20} sts on first needle and 16{17-19} sts on third needle.

Instructions continued on page 22.

Rnds 3 thru 12{12-14}: Repeat Rnds 1 and 2, 5{5-6} times: 12{13-14} sts on first needle, 25{27-29} sts on second needle, and 11{12-13} sts on third needle for a total of 48{52-56} sts.

FOOT

Work even until Foot measures approximately 3" (7.5 cm) less than desired finished foot length, ending by working Row 2 or 4 of Cable Panel *(see Sizing, page 86)*.

Next Rnd: Knit across to first marker, remove marker, K4, P1, K2, [slip 1 as if to **knit**, K2 tog, PSSO *(Fig. 10, page 90)*], K2, P1, K4, remove marker, knit across: 23{25-27} sts on second needle for a total of 46{50-54} sts.

Knit every round until Foot measures approximately 2¼{2¼-2½}"/5.5{5.5-6.5} cm less than desired finished foot length.

TOE

Rnd 1 (Decrease rnd): Knit across first needle to last 3 sts, K2 tog, K1; on second needle K1, SSK, knit across to last 3 sts, K2 tog, K1; on third needle K1, SSK, knit across: 42{46-50} sts.

Rnd 2: Knit around.

Rnds 3 thru 15{15-17}: Repeat Rnds 1 and 2, 6{6-7} times, then repeat Rnd 1 once **more**: 4{5-5} sts on first needle, 7{9-9} sts on second needle and 3{4-4} sts on third needle for a total of 14{18-18} sts.

Knit across the sts on first needle. Slip the sts from the third needle onto the first needle. There should be 7{9-9} sts on both needles.

Cut yarn leaving a 12" (30.5 cm) end. Thread tapestry needle with end and graft the remaining stitches together *(Figs. 14a & b, page 91)*.

Repeat for second Sock.

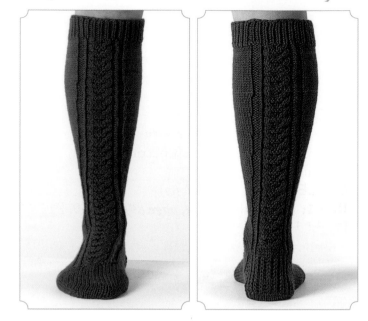

{ LADDER CABLES }

Finished Calf Circumference:
12¼{13¾-15½}"/31{35-39.5} cm

Size Note: The Cable Panels have a lot of stretch. For a good fit, choose your size based on a calf circumference of up to 1½" to 2" (4 to 5 cm) less than your actual calf measurement. Instructions are written for 12¼" circumference with 13¾" and 15½" circumferences in braces { }. Instructions will be easier to read if you circle all the numbers pertaining to your size. If only one number is given, it applies to all sizes.

MATERIALS
Medium Weight Yarn **MEDIUM 4**
[1.75 ounces, 110 yards
(50 grams, 101 meters) per skein]:
4{4-5} skeins
Set of 5 double pointed needles,
size 7 (4.5 mm) **or** size needed for gauge
Cable needle
Split-ring markers - 3
Stitch holder
Yarn needle

GAUGE: In Stockinette Stitch,
20 sts and 26 rows = 4" (10 cm)
Cable Panel, 17 sts = 2½" (6.25 cm)
unblocked

STITCH GUIDE

BACK CABLE (uses 4 sts)
Slip next 2 sts onto cable needle and hold in **back** of work, K2 from left needle, K2 from cable needle.

FRONT CABLE (uses 4 sts)
Slip next 2 sts onto cable needle and hold in **front** of work, K2 from left needle, K2 from cable needle.

CABLE PANEL (uses 17 sts)
Row 1: P2, K1 tbl *(Fig. 4, page 89)*, P1, K9, P1, K1 tbl, P2.
Row 2: P2, K1 tbl, P1, Front Cable, K1, Back Cable, P1, K1 tbl, P2.
Row 3: P2, K1 tbl, P1, K2, P5, K2, P1, K1 tbl, P2.
Rows 4 and 5: P2, K1 tbl, P1, K9, P1, K1 tbl, P2.
Repeat Rows 2-5 for Cable Panel.

CUFF

Cast on 66{74-82} sts.

Divide sts onto 4 needles *(see Double Pointed Needles, page 88)*, placing 16{18-20} sts on first needle, 17{19-21} sts on second needle, 16{18-20} sts on third needle, and 17{19-21} sts on fourth needle.

Place a split-ring marker around the first stitch to indicate the beginning of the round *(see Markers, page 88)*.

Work in K1, P1 ribbing for 1¹/₂" (4 cm).

LEG

Rearrange the sts, slipping 1{3-5} st(s) from first needle onto second needle and 1{3-5} st(s) from third needle onto fourth needle: 15 sts on first and third needles and 18{22-26} sts on second and fourth needles.

Increase Rnd: ★ P2, (K1, P1) twice, M1 *(Figs. 6a & b, page 89)*, K3, M1, (P1, K1) twice, P2, knit across next needle; repeat from ★ once **more**: 17 sts on first and third needles for a total of 70{78-86} sts.

Rnd 1: Work Cable Panel, knit across second needle, work Cable Panel, knit across.

Repeat Rnd 1 for pattern until Sock measures approximately 4" (10 cm) from cast on edge.

Decrease Rnd: ★ Work Cable Panel, K2 tog *(Fig. 7, page 89)*, knit across to last 2 sts on same needle, SSK *(Figs. 9a-c, page 90)*; repeat from ★ once **more**: 66{74-82} sts.

Continuing in established pattern, repeat decrease round every eighth round, 5{6-7} times: 6{8-10} sts on second and fourth needles for a total of 46{50-54} sts.

Work even until Sock measures approximately 13{13³/₄-14¹/₂}"/33{35-37} cm from cast on edge **or** desired length to top of heel, ending by working Row 1 of Cable Panel.

HEEL & GUSSET

Work same as Annelise Crossed Cable, page 21.

FOOT

Work even until Foot measures approximately 3" (7.5 cm) less than desired finished foot length, ending by working Row 2 of Cable Panel *(see Sizing, page 86)*.

Next Rnd: Knit across to first marker, remove marker, K4, P2, SSK, K1, K2 tog, P2, K4, remove marker, knit across: 23{25-27} sts on second needle for a total of 46{50-54} sts.

Knit every round until Foot measures approximately 2¹/₄{2¹/₄-2¹/₂}"/5.5{5.5-6.5} cm less than desired finished foot length.

Beginning with Toe, complete same as Annelise Crossed Cables, page 22.

Repeat for second Sock.

EMMA LACE SOCKS

 **INTERMEDIATE**

Finished Ankle Circumference: 8" (20.5 cm)

Size Note: The lace pattern has a good deal of stretch, and should fit an ankle up to 9" (23 cm). A smaller sock can be produced by knitting at a tighter gauge.

MATERIALS

Super Fine Weight Yarn
[2 ounces, 215 yards
(60 grams, 197 meters) per hank]: 2 hanks
Set of 4 double pointed needles,
size 2 (2.75 mm) **or** size needed for gauge
Split-ring marker
Stitch holder
Tapestry needle

GAUGE: In Stockinette Stitch,
32 sts and 44 rows = 4" (10 cm)
in Perforated Stripes pattern,
30 sts and 44 rows = 4" (10 cm)

Gauge Swatch: 4" (10 cm)
Cast on 30 sts.
Row 1: Purl across.
Row 2: K2, YO *(Fig. 5, page 89)*, K2 tog *(Fig. 7, page 89)*, ★ K3, YO, K2 tog; repeat from ★ across to last st, K1.
Row 3: Purl across.
Row 4: K2, K2 tog, YO, ★ K3, K2 tog, YO; repeat from ★ across to last st, K1.
Rows 5-44: Repeat Rows 1-4, 10 times.
Bind off all sts.

CUFF

Cast on 72 sts.

Divide sts onto 3 needles *(see Double Pointed Needles, page 88)*, placing 24 sts on each needle.

Place a split-ring marker around the first stitch to indicate the beginning of the round *(see Markers, page 88)*.

Rnd 1: Knit around.

Rnd 2: Purl around.

Rnd 3: Knit around.

Rnd 4: K3, P7, ★ K5, P7; repeat from ★ around to last 2 sts, K2.

Rnd 5: ★ K1, SSK *(Figs. 9a-c, page 90)*, K7, K2 tog *(Fig. 7, page 89)*; repeat from ★ around: 20 sts on each needle.

Rnd 6: ★ K1, SSK, K5, K2 tog; repeat from ★ around: 16 sts on each needle.

Rnd 7: K3, (YO, K1) 3 times *(Fig. 5, page 89)*, YO, ★ K5, (YO, K1) 3 times, YO; repeat from ★ around to last 2 sts, K2: 24 sts on each needle.

Instructions continue on page 26.

Rnds 8-21: Repeat Rnds 4-7, 3 times; then repeat Rnds 4 and 5 once **more** for Fan Shell pattern: 20 sts on each needle.

Rnd 22: Purl around.

Rnd 23: ★ YO, K2 tog; repeat from ★ around.

Rnd 24: Purl around.

LEG

Rnd 1: K2, YO, K2 tog, ★ K3, YO, K2 tog; repeat from ★ around to last st, K1.

Rnd 2: Knit around.

Rnd 3: K2, K2 tog, YO, ★ K3, K2 tog, YO; repeat from ★ around to last st, K1.

Rnd 4: Knit around.

Repeat Rnds 1-4 for Perforated Stripes pattern until Sock measures approximately 8" (20.5 cm) from cast on edge **or** to desired length to top of heel, ending by working Rnd 4.

HEEL

Dividing Stitches: Slip first 11 sts from second needle onto first needle. Remove marker. The Heel Flap will be worked back and forth across these 31 sts.

Slip the remaining 29 sts onto a st holder for Instep to be worked later.

HEEL FLAP

When instructed to **slip a stitch** while working the Heel (that is not part of an SSK decrease), slip as if to **purl** with yarn held to **wrong** side. (On **right** side rows, the yarn will be held at the **back** of work and on **wrong** side rows, the yarn will be held at the **front** of work.) This will prevent twisted stitches and also prevent the working yarn from showing on the right side.

Row 1: Slip 1, K1, YO, K2 tog, knit across to last 4 sts, YO, K2 tog, K1, P1.

Row 2: Slip 1, purl across.

Row 3: Slip 1, K1, K2 tog, YO, knit across to last 4 sts, K2 tog, YO, K1, P1.

Row 4: Slip 1, purl across.

Rows 5-24: Repeat Rows 1-4, 5 times.

Row 25: Slip 1, knit across.

Row 26: Slip 1, purl across.

Rows 27-31: Repeat Rows 25 and 26 twice, then repeat Row 25 once **more**.

TURNING HEEL

Begin working short rows as follows:

Row 1: P 18, P2 tog *(Fig. 12, page 91)*, P1, leave remaining 10 sts unworked; **turn**.

Row 2: Slip 1, K6, SSK, K1, leave remaining 10 sts unworked; turn.

Row 3: Slip 1, P7, P2 tog, P1; turn.

Row 4: Slip 1, K8, SSK, K1; turn.

Row 5: Slip 1, P9, P2 tog, P1; turn.

Row 6: Slip 1, K 10, SSK, K1; turn.

Row 7: Slip 1, P 11, P2 tog, P1; turn.

Row 8: Slip 1, K 12, SSK, K1; turn.

Row 9: Slip 1, P 13, P2 tog, P1; turn.

Row 10: Slip 1, K 14, SSK, K1; turn.

Row 11: Slip 1, P 15, P2 tog, P1; turn.

Row 12: Slip 1, K 16, SSK, K1; do **not** turn: 19 sts.

GUSSET

The remainder of the Sock is worked in rounds.

Slip the Instep sts from the st holder onto an empty needle.

FOUNDATION ROUND

With **right** side of Heel facing, continue with the working yarn and the needle that is holding the Heel sts and pick up 15 sts along the side of the Heel Flap *(Fig. 13, page 91)*.

With an empty needle and working across Instep sts, K1, YO, K2 tog, (K3, YO, K2 tog) 5 times, K1.

With an empty needle, pick up 15 sts along the side of the Heel Flap, then knit the first 9 Heel sts; place a marker around the first st on the next needle to indicate the beginning of the round.

There should be 25 sts on first needle, 29 sts on second needle, and 24 sts on third needle for a total of 78 sts.

GUSSET DECREASES

Rnd 1 (Decrease rnd): Knit across to last 3 sts on first needle, K2 tog, K1; knit across second needle; on third needle, K1, SSK, knit across: 76 sts.

Rnd 2: Knit across first needle; on second needle, K1, K2 tog, YO, (K3, K2 tog, YO) 5 times, K1; knit across third needle.

Rnd 3 (Decrease rnd): Knit across to last 3 sts on first needle, K2 tog, K1; knit across second needle; on third needle, K1, SSK, knit across: 74 sts.

Rnd 4: Knit across first needle; on second needle, K1, YO, K2 tog, (K3, YO, K2 tog) 5 times, K1; knit across third needle.

Rnds 5-17: Repeat Rnds 1-4, 3 times; then repeat Rnd 1 once **more**: 16 sts on first needle, 29 sts on second needle, and 15 sts on third needle for a total of 60 sts.

FOOT

Work even until Foot measures approximately 2" (5 cm) less than desired finished foot length *(see Sizing, page 86)*.

TOE

Slip first 4 sts from second needle onto first needle and last 5 sts from second needle onto third needle, so that there are 20 sts on each needle.

Rnds 1-4: Knit around.

Rnd 5: ★ K1, SSK, K5, K2 tog; repeat from ★ around: 48 sts.

Rnds 6-12: Knit around.

Rnd 13: ★ K1, SSK, K3, K2 tog; repeat from ★ around: 36 sts.

Rnds 14-18: Knit around.

Rnd 19: ★ K1, SSK, K1, K2 tog; repeat from ★ around: 24 sts.

Rnds 20-22: Knit around.

Rnd 23: ★ K1, [slip 1 as if to **knit**, K2 tog, PSSO *(Fig. 10, page 90)*]; repeat from ★ around: 12 sts.

Rnd 24: Knit around.

Cut yarn leaving a 9" (23 cm) end for sewing. Thread tapestry needle with end and slip remaining sts onto tapestry needle; gather tightly to close and secure end.

Repeat for second Sock.

IRIS SOCKS

These socks avoid shaping in the color work pattern by using a Band Heel. This is similar to a standard heel, but instead of working a gusset after stitches are picked up from the Heel Flap, the decreases are worked as part of the Heel.

◼◼◼◼◻ **INTERMEDIATE**

Finished Ankle Circumference:
7{8-9}"/18{20.5-23} cm

Size Note: Instructions are written for 7" circumference with 8" and 9" circumferences in braces { }. Instructions will be easier to read if you circle all the numbers pertaining to your size. If only one number is given, it applies to all sizes.

MATERIALS
Super Fine Weight Yarn
[3.5 ounces, 437 yards
(100 grams, 400 meters) per hank]:
  MC (Blue) - 1 hank
  CC (Lt Blue) - 1 hank
Note: If substituting yarn, allow approximately 120 to 150 yards (110 to 137 meters) of CC.
Set of 5 double pointed needles,
  size 2 (2.75 mm) **or** size needed for gauge
Split-ring marker
Stitch holder
Tapestry needle

GAUGE: In Stockinette Stitch, in color pattern,
    36 sts = 4" (10 cm)

CUFF
With MC, cast on 56{64-72} sts.

Divide sts onto 4 needles *(see Double Pointed Needles, page 88)*, placing 14{16-18} sts on each needle.

Place a split-ring marker around the first stitch to indicate the beginning of the round *(see Markers, page 88)*.

Work in K2, P2 ribbing for 5½" (14 cm).

LEG
Rnd 1: Knit around.

Note: When working M1 increase *(Figs. 6a & b, page 89)* between needles, place new stitch on same needle as last stitch made.

Rnd 2 (Increase rnd): ★ K7{8-9}, M1; repeat from ★ around: 16{18-20} sts on each needle for a total of 64{72-80} sts.

Rnd 3: Knit around.

Instructions continue on page 30.

Rnds 4-19: Knit around, following Ankle Chart for 16 rnds *(see Fair Isle Knitting, page 92)*.

Cut MC and CC.

ANKLE CHART

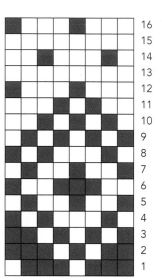

KEY

■ - MC
□ - CC

Follow chart from right to left and from bottom to top.

HEEL

Dividing Stitches: Slip 16{18-20} sts from fourth needle onto first needle. Remove marker. Using MC, the Heel Flap will be worked back and forth across these 32{36-40} sts beginning with a **right** side row.

Slip the remaining 32{36-40} sts onto a st holder for Instep to be worked later.

HEEL FLAP

When instructed to **slip a stitch** while working the Heel (that is not part of an SSK decrease), slip as if to **purl** with yarn held to **wrong** side. (On **right** side rows, the yarn will be held at the **back** of work and on **wrong** side rows, the yarn will be held at the **front** of work.) This will prevent twisted stitches and also prevent the working yarn from showing on the right side.

Row 1: Slip 1, knit across.

Row 2: Slip 1, purl across.

Rows 3 thru 16{18-20}: Repeat Rows 1 and 2, 7{8-9} times.

HEEL BAND SHAPING

Row 1: Slip 1, K 10{11-12}, K2 tog *(Fig. 7, page 89)*, K6{8-10}, SSK *(Figs. 9a-c, page 90)*, K 11{12-13}: 30{34-38} sts.

Row 2: Slip 1, purl across.

Row 3: Slip 1, K 9{10-11}, K2 tog, K6{8-10}, SSK, K 10{11-12}: 28{32-36} sts.

Row 4: Slip 1, purl across.

Row 5: Slip 1, K8{9-10}, K2 tog, K6{8-10}, SSK, K 9{10-11}: 26{30-34} sts.

Row 6: Slip 1, purl across.

Row 7: Slip 1, K7{8-9}, K2 tog, K6{8-10}, SSK, K 8{9-10}: 24{28-32} sts.

Row 8: Slip 1, purl across.

TURNING HEEL

Begin working short rows as follows:

Row 1: Slip 1, K 14{17-20}, SSK, leave remaining 7{8-9} sts unworked; **turn**.

Row 2: Slip 1, P6{8-10}, P2 tog *(Fig. 12, page 91)*, leave remaining 7{8-9} sts unworked; turn.

Row 3: Slip 1, K6{8-10}, SSK; turn.

Row 4: Slip 1, P6{8-10}, P2 tog; turn.

Rows 5 thru 16{18-20}: Repeat Rows 3 and 4, 6{7-8} times: 8{10-12} sts.

FOOT
FOUNDATION ROUND

The remainder of the Sock is worked in rounds. Gusset Shaping is not needed in this style.

Slip the Instep sts from the st holder onto an empty needle.

With **right** side of Heel facing, continue with the working yarn and the needle that is holding the Heel sts, K4{5-6}, drop yarn; place a marker around the next st to indicate the beginning of the round.

With an empty needle and CC, knit the remaining 4{5-6} sts, then pick up 12{13-14} sts along the side of the Heel Flap *(Fig. 13, page 91)*.

With an empty needle, knit the first 16{18-20} Instep sts (Foot Chart Row 1).

With an empty needle, knit the remaining 16{18-20} Instep sts.

With an empty needle, pick up 12{13-14} sts along the side of the Heel Flap, then knit 4{5-6} Heel sts.

There should be 16{18-20} sts on each needle for a total of 64{72-80} sts.

Beginning with Row 2, follow Rows 1-4 of Foot Chart until Foot measures approximately 2¼" (5.5 cm) less than desired finished foot length *(see Sizing, page 86)*, ending by working Row 4.

FOOT CHART

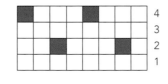

KEY
■ - MC
□ - CC

Follow chart from right to left and from bottom to top.

TOE

Rnds 1-9: Knit around following Toe Chart for 9 rnds.

Cut CC.

TOE CHART

KEY
■ - MC
□ - CC

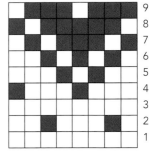

Follow chart from right to left and from bottom to top.

Rnds 10 and 11: With MC, knit around.

Rnd 12: K2, [slip 2 together as if to **knit**, K1, P2SSO *(Fig. 11, page 90)*], ★ K5, slip 2 together as if to **knit**, K1, P2SSO; repeat from ★ around to last 3 sts, K3: 48{54-60} sts.

Rnds 13-16: Knit around.

Rnd 17: K1, slip 2 together as if to **knit**, K1, P2SSO, ★ K3, slip 2 together as if to **knit**, K1, P2SSO; repeat from ★ around to last 2 sts, K2: 32{36-40} sts.

Rnds 18-20: Knit around.

Rnd 21: ★ Slip 2 together as if to **knit**, K1, P2SSO, K1; repeat from ★ around: 16{18-20} sts.

Rnds 22-24: Knit around.

Rnd 25: K2 tog around: 8{9-10} sts.

Cut yarn leaving a 9" (23 cm) end for sewing. Thread tapestry needle with end and slip remaining sts onto tapestry needle; gather tightly to close and secure end.

Repeat for second Sock.

LUCY ANKLET SOCKS

The Lucy Socks make the perfect feminine ankle sock, featuring three lacy cuffs. Choose from ZigZag Eyelet Cuff, Eyelet Rib Cuff on page 36, or Little Fountains Cuff on page 37.

{ZIGZAG EYELET CUFF}

Finished Ankle Circumference: 7¹/₂{9}"/19{23} cm

Size Note: Instructions are written for 7¹/₂" circumference with 9" circumference in braces { }. Instructions will be easier to read if you circle all the numbers pertaining to your size. If only one number is given, it applies to both sizes.

MATERIALS
Super Fine Weight Yarn
　[3.5 ounces, 438 yards
　(100 grams, 400 meters) per skein]:
　　1 skein
Set of 5 double pointed needles,
　size 2 (2.75 mm) **or** size needed for gauge
Split-ring marker
Stitch holder
Tapestry needle

GAUGE: In Stockinette Stitch,
　　　32 sts and 44 rows = 4" (10 cm)

CUFF
Cast on 60{72} sts.

Divide sts onto 4 needles as follows *(see Double Pointed Needles, page 88)*: 12{18} sts on first needle, 18 sts on second needle, 12{18} sts on third needle, and 18 sts on fourth needle.

Place a split-ring marker around the first stitch to indicate the beginning of the round *(see Markers, page 88)*.

Rnds 1-3: Knit around.

Rnd 4: Purl around.

Rnd 5: Knit around.

Rnd 6: Purl around.

Rnd 7: K2, K2 tog *(Fig. 7, page 89)*, YO *(Fig. 5, page 89)*, ★ K4, K2 tog, YO; repeat from ★ around to last 2 sts, K2.

Rnd 8 AND ALL EVEN NUMBERED RNDS: Knit around.

Rnd 9: K1, K2 tog, YO, ★ K4, K2 tog, YO; repeat from ★ around to last 3 sts, K3.

Rnd 11: ★ K2 tog, YO, K4; repeat from ★ around.

Rnd 13: K2, YO, SSK *(Figs. 9a-c, page 90)*, ★ K4, YO, SSK; repeat from ★ around to last 2 sts, K2.

Instructions continue on page 34.

Rnd 15: K3, YO, SSK, ★ K4, YO, SSK; repeat from ★ around to last st, K1.

Rnd 17: ★ K4, YO, SSK; repeat from ★ around.

Rnds 19-36: Repeat Rnds 7-18 once, then repeat Rnds 7-12 once **more** for Zigzag Eyelet pattern.

Rnd 37 (Turning ridge): Purl around.

Rnd 38: Knit around.

Rnd 39: Purl around.

Rnds 40-43: Knit around.

LEG
Flip the needles upside down and rotate the Cuff stitches, so that the Sock is inside out with the purl side facing outwards. To prevent a hole at the beginning of the round, bring the working yarn to the back, slip the last stitch on the right needle onto the left needle, bring the yarn to the front and return the slipped stitch to the right needle; bring the yarn to the back.
Move the marker to the first stitch on the left needle.

Rnds 1-11: ★ K3, P1; repeat from ★ around.

First Size (7¹⁄₂") Only: Slip 3 sts from first needle onto second needle and 3 sts from third needle onto fourth needle, so there are 15 sts on each needle.

Both Sizes - Rnds 12-30: Knit around.

HEEL
Dividing Stitches: Slip all of the sts from second needle and one st from third needle onto first needle. Remove marker. The Heel Flap will be worked back and forth across these 31{37} sts.

Slip the remaining 29{35} sts onto a st holder for Instep to be worked later.

HEEL FLAP

When instructed to **slip a stitch** (that is not part of an SSK decrease), slip as if to **purl** with yarn held to **wrong** side. (On **right** side rows, the yarn will be held at the **back** of work and on **wrong** side rows, the yarn will be held at the **front** of work.) This will prevent twisted stitches and also prevent the working yarn from showing on the right side.

Row 1: Knit across.

Row 2: Purl across.

Row 3: Slip 1, ★ K2, slip 1; repeat from ★ across.

Rows 4 thru 29{35}: Repeat Rows 2 and 3, 13{16} times.

TURNING HEEL
Begin working short rows as follows:

Row 1: P 18{21}, P2 tog *(Fig. 12, page 91)*, P1, leave remaining 10{13} sts unworked; **turn.**

Row 2: Slip 1, K6, SSK, K1, leave remaining 10{13} sts unworked; turn.

Row 3: Slip 1, P7, P2 tog, P1; turn.

Row 4: Slip 1, K8, SSK, K1; turn.

Row 5: Slip 1, P9, P2 tog, P1; turn.

Row 6: Slip 1, K 10, SSK, K1; turn.

Row 7: Slip 1, P 11, P2 tog, P1; turn.

Row 8: Slip 1, K 12, SSK, K1; turn.

Row 9: Slip 1, P 13, P2 tog, P1; turn.

Row 10: Slip 1, K 14, SSK, K1; turn.

Row 11: Slip 1, P 15, P2 tog, P1; turn.

FIRST SIZE (7¹/₂") ONLY
Row 12: Slip 1, K 16, SSK, K1; do **not** turn: 19 sts.

SECOND SIZE (9") ONLY
Row 12: Slip 1, K 16, SSK, K1; turn.

Row 13: Slip 1, P 17, P2 tog, P1; turn.

Row 14: Slip 1, K 18, SSK, K1; turn.

Row 15: Slip 1, P 19, P2 tog; turn.

Row 16: Slip 1, K 19, SSK; do **not** turn: 21 sts.

GUSSET

The remainder of the Sock is worked in rounds.

Slip the Instep sts from the st holder onto an empty needle.

FOUNDATION ROUND

With **right** side of Heel facing, continue with the working yarn and the needle that is holding the Heel sts and pick up 14{17} sts along the side of the Heel Flap and one st in the corner (where the Heel Flap meets the Instep) *(Fig. 13, page 91)*.

With an empty needle, knit the first 14{17} Instep sts.

With an empty needle, knit the remaining 15{18} Instep sts.

With an empty needle, pick up one st in the corner and 14{17} sts along the side of the Heel Flap, then knit the first 9{10} Heel sts; place a marker around the first st on the next needle to indicate the beginning of the round.

There should be 25{29} sts on first needle, 14{17} sts on second needle, 15{18} sts on third needle, and 24{28} sts on fourth needle for a total of 78{92} sts.

GUSSET DECREASES
Rnd 1: Knit around.

Rnd 2 (Decrease rnd)**:** Knit across to last 3 sts on first needle, K2 tog, K1; knit across second and third needles; on fourth needle K1, SSK, knit across: 76{90} sts.

Rnds 3 thru 18{20}: Repeat Rnds 1 and 2, 8{9} times: 16{19} sts on first needle and 15{18} sts on fourth needle.

Slip the last stitch on the first needle onto second needle. There should now be 15{18} sts on each needle for a total of 60{72} sts.

FOOT
Knit every round until Foot measures approximately 2" (5 cm) less than desired finished foot length *(see Sizing, page 86)*.

TOE
Rnd 1: Knit across to fourth needle; move beginning marker to first st on fourth needle. This is now the beginning of the round.

Rnd 2 (Decrease rnd)**:** K1, SSK, knit across first needle; knit across second needle to last 3 sts, K2 tog, K1; on third needle K1, SSK, knit across; knit across fourth needle to last 3 sts, K2 tog, K1: 14{17} sts each needle.

Rnd 3: Knit around.

Rnds 4 thru 17{19}: Repeat Rnds 2 and 3, 7{8} times: 7{9} sts on each needle for a total of 28{36} sts.

Rnds 18{20} thru 20{22}: Repeat Rnd 2, 3 times: 4{6} sts on each needle for a total of 16{24} sts.

Slip the sts from second needle onto first needle. Slip the sts from fourth needle onto third needle.

Cut yarn leaving a 12" (30.5 cm) end. Thread tapestry needle with end and graft the remaining stitches together *(Figs. 14a & b, page 91)*.

Repeat for second Sock.

{EYELET RIB CUFF}

Finished Ankle Circumference: 7¹/₂{9}"/19{23} cm

Size Note: Instructions are written for 7¹/₂"
circumference with 9" circumference in braces { }.
Instructions will be easier to read if you circle all the
numbers pertaining to your size. If only one number
is given, it applies to both sizes.

MATERIALS

Super Fine Weight Yarn
[1.75 ounces, 231 yards
(50 grams, 211 meters) per skein]: 2 skeins
Set of 5 double pointed needles,
size 2 (2.75 mm) **or** size needed for gauge
Split-ring marker
Stitch holder
Tapestry needle

GAUGE: In Stockinette Stitch,
32 sts and 44 rows = 4" (10 cm)

CUFF

Cast on 60{72} sts.

Divide sts onto 4 needles as follows *(see Double
Pointed Needles, page 88)*: 12{18} sts on first needle,
18 sts on second needle, 12{18} sts on third needle,
and 18 sts on fourth needle.

Place a split-ring marker around the first stitch to
indicate the beginning of the round *(see Markers,
page 88)*.

Rnds 1 and 2: Knit around.

Rnds 3 and 4: ★ P1, K5; repeat from ★ around.

Rnd 5: ★ P1, K2 tog *(Fig. 7, page 89)*, YO *(Fig. 5,
page 89)*, K1, YO, SSK *(Figs. 9a-c, page 90)*; repeat
from ★ around.

Rnds 6-8: ★ P1, K5; repeat from ★ around.

Rnd 9: ★ P1, K2 tog, YO, K1, YO, SSK; repeat
from ★ around.

Rnds 10-34: Repeat Rnds 6-9, 6 times; then repeat
Rnd 6 once **more** for Eyelet Rib pattern.

Rnd 35 (Turning ridge)**:** Purl around.

Rnds 36-39: Knit around.

LEG

Flip the needles upside down and rotate the Cuff
stitches, so that the Sock is inside out with the
purl side facing outwards. To prevent a hole at the
beginning of the round, bring the working yarn
to the back, slip the last stitch on the right needle
onto the left needle, bring the yarn to the front and
return the slipped stitch to the right needle; bring
the yarn to the back.
Move the marker to the first stitch on the left
needle.

Rnds 1-11: ★ K3, P1; repeat from ★ around.

First Size (7¹/₂") Only: Slip 3 sts from first needle
onto second needle and 3 sts from third needle onto
fourth needle, so there are 15 sts on each needle.

Both Sizes - Rnds 12-27: Knit around.

Beginning with Heel, complete same as Lucy
Zigzag Eyelet Cuff, page 34.

Repeat for second Sock.

{LITTLE FOUNTAINS CUFF}

Finished Ankle Circumference: 7¹/₂{9}"/19{23} cm

Size Note: Instructions are written for 7¹/₂"
circumference with 9" circumference in braces { }.
Instructions will be easier to read if you circle all the
numbers pertaining to your size. If only one number
is given, it applies to both sizes.

MATERIALS

Super Fine Weight Yarn
[2 ounces, 215 yards
(60 grams, 197 meters) per hank]: 2 hanks
Set of 5 double pointed needles,
size 2 (2.75 mm) **or** size needed for gauge
Split-ring marker
Stitch holder
Tapestry needle

GAUGE: In Stockinette Stitch,
32 sts and 44 rows = 4" (10 cm)

CUFF

Cast on 60{72} sts.

Divide sts onto 4 needles as follows *(see Double
Pointed Needles, page 88)*: 12{18} sts on first needle,
18 sts on second needle, 12{18} sts on third needle,
and 18 sts on fourth needle.

Place a split-ring marker around the first stitch to
indicate the beginning of the round *(see Markers,
page 88)*.

Rnd 1: Knit around.

Rnd 2: K2, [slip 1 as if to **knit**, K2 tog, PSSO
(Fig. 10, page 90)], ★ K3, slip 1 as if to **knit**, K2 tog,
PSSO; repeat from ★ around to last st, K1: 40{48} sts.

Rnd 3: Knit around.

To return to the same stitch count on each needle
as on Rnd 1, when you reach the end of the needle,
place the next yarn over onto the right needle before
working across the next needle.

Rnd 4: ★ K1, YO *(Fig. 5, page 89)*, K3, YO; repeat
from ★ around: 60{72} sts.

Rnds 5-32: Repeat Rnds 1-4, 7 times for Little
Fountains pattern.

Rnd 33: Knit around.

Rnd 34 (Turning ridge): Purl around.

Rnds 35-38: Knit around.

LEG

Flip the needles upside down and rotate the Cuff
stitches, so that the Sock is inside out with the
purl side facing outwards. To prevent a hole at the
beginning of the round, bring the working yarn to
the back, slip the last stitch on the right needle onto
the left needle, bring the yarn to the front and return
the slipped stitch to the right needle; bring the yarn
to the back.
Move the marker to the first stitch on the left needle.

Rnds 1-11: ★ K3, P1; repeat from ★ around.

First Size (7¹/₂") Only: Slip 3 sts from first needle
onto second needle and 3 sts from third needle onto
fourth needle, so there are 15 sts on each needle.

Both Sizes - Rnds 12-27: Knit around.

Beginning with Heel, complete same as Lucy Zigzag
Eyelet Cuff, page 34.

Repeat for second Sock.

IVY SOCKS

 **INTERMEDIATE**

Finished Cuff Circumference:
7³/₄{8³/₄-10}"/19.5{22-25.5} cm

Size Note: The color stranded knitting used on the cuff of this pattern has less widthwise stretch than the ribbing. For a good fit, choose your size based on leg measurement at cuff. While standing, measure your leg circumference about 7¹/₂{8-8¹/₂}"/19{20.5-21.5} cm from the floor. The finished size should be the same or ³/₄" (2 cm) smaller than your actual leg measurement. Instructions are written for 7³/₄" circumference with 8³/₄", and 10" circumferences in braces { }. Instructions will be easier to read if you circle all the numbers pertaining to your size. If only one number is given, it applies to all sizes.

MATERIALS

Super Fine Weight Yarn
  [3.5 ounces, 437 yards
   (100 grams, 400 meters) per skein]:
    MC (Green) - 1 hank
    CC (White) - 1 hank or approximately
     70 yards (64 meters)
Set of 5 double pointed needles,
  size 2 (2.75 mm) **or** size needed for gauge
Split-ring marker
Stitch holder
Tapestry needle

GAUGE: In Stockinette Stitch,
    32 sts and 44 rows = 4" (10 cm)
    in color pattern, 36 sts = 4" (10 cm)

CUFF
With MC, cast on 56{64-72} sts.

Divide sts onto 4 needles, placing 14{16-18} sts on each needle *(see Double Pointed Needles, page 88)*.

Place a split-ring marker around the first stitch to indicate the beginning of the round *(see Markers, page 88)*.

Rnds 1-11: ★ K3, P1; repeat from ★ around.

Rnd 12: With CC, knit around.

Note: When working M1 increase *(Figs. 6a & b, page 89)* between needles, place new stitch on same needle as last stitch made.

Rnd 13 (Increase rnd): ★ K4, M1; repeat from ★ around: 70{80-90} sts.

Rnds 14-28: Knit around following Rows 1-15 of Ivy Chart, *(see Fair Isle Knitting, page 92)*.

IVY CHART

KEY
■ - MC
□ - CC

Follow chart from right to left and from bottom to top.

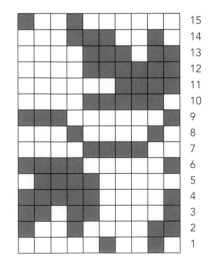

Instructions continue on page 40.

Rnd 29: With CC, knit around.

Rnd 30 (Decrease rnd): ★ K3, K2 tog *(Fig. 7, page 89)*; repeat from ★ around: 14{16-18} sts on each needle for a total of 56{64-72} sts.

Rnd 31: Cut CC; with MC, knit around.

LEG

Work in K3, P1 ribbing until Sock measures approximately 6³⁄₄{7-7¹⁄₄}"/17{18-18.5} cm from cast on edge **or** to desired length to top of heel.

HEEL

Dividing Stitches: Work in pattern across to last st on third needle. Slip last st onto fourth needle, remove marker, then slip 14{16-18} sts from first needle onto fourth needle. The Heel Flap will be worked back and forth across these 29{33-37} sts.

Slip the remaining 27{31-35} sts onto a st holder for Instep to be worked later.

HEEL FLAP

When instructed to **slip a stitch**, slip as if to **purl** with yarn held to **wrong** side so that the working yarn won't show, unless otherwise indicated. (On **right** side rows, the yarn will be held at the **back** of work and on **wrong** side rows, the yarn will be held at the **front** of work.)

Row 1: Slip 1, ★ K1, slip 1; repeat from ★ across.

Row 2: Purl across.

Row 3: Slip 1, K2, slip 1, ★ K1, slip 1; repeat from ★ across to last 3 sts, K2, slip 1.

Row 4: Purl across.

Rows 5 thru 28{32-36}: Repeat Rows 1-4, 6{7-8} times.

TURNING HEEL

Begin working short rows as follows:

Row 1: Slip 1, K 16{18-20}, SSK *(Figs. 9a-c, page 90)*, K1, leave remaining 9{11-13} sts unworked; **turn**.

Row 2: Slip 1, P6, P2 tog *(Fig. 12, page 91)*, P1, leave remaining 9{11-13} sts unworked; turn.

Row 3: Slip 1, K7, SSK, K1; turn.

Row 4: Slip 1, P8, P2 tog, P1; turn.

Row 5: Slip 1, K9, SSK, K1; turn.

Row 6: Slip 1, P 10, P2 tog, P1; turn.

Row 7: Slip 1, K 11, SSK, K1; turn.

Row 8: Slip 1, P 12, P2 tog, P1; turn.

Row 9: Slip 1, K 13, SSK, K1; turn.

Row 10: Slip 1, P 14, P2 tog, P1; turn.

FIRST SIZE (7³⁄₄") ONLY
Row 11: Slip 1, K 15, SSK; turn.

Row 12: Slip 1, P 15, P2 tog; turn: 17 sts.

SECOND SIZE (8³⁄₄") ONLY
Row 11: Slip 1, K 15, SSK, K1; turn.

Row 12: Slip 1, P 16, P2 tog, P1; turn.

Row 13: Slip 1, K 17, SSK; turn.

Row 14: Slip 1, P 17, P2 tog; turn: 19 sts.

THIRD SIZE (10") ONLY
Row 11: Slip 1, K 15, SSK, K1; turn.

Row 12: Slip 1, P 16, P2 tog, P1; turn.

Row 13: Slip 1, K 17, SSK, K1; turn.

Row 14: Slip 1, P 18, P2 tog, P1; turn.

Row 15: Slip 1, K 19, SSK; turn.

Row 16: Slip 1, P 19, P2 tog; turn: 21 sts.

GUSSET

The remainder of the Sock is worked in rounds.

Slip the Instep sts from the st holder onto an empty needle.

FOUNDATION ROUND

With **right** side of Heel facing, continue with the working yarn and the needle that is holding the Heel sts, K9{10-11}; place a marker around the next st to indicate the beginning of the round.

With an empty needle, knit the remaining 8{9-10} sts, then pick up 14{16-18} sts along the side of the Heel Flap and one st in the corner (where the Heel Flap meets the Instep) *(Fig. 13, page 91)*.

With an empty needle, work the first 14{16-18} Instep sts in established rib pattern.

With an empty needle, work the remaining 13{15-17} Instep sts in established rib pattern.

With an empty needle, pick up one st in the corner and 14{16-18} sts along the side of the Heel Flap, then knit the first 9{10-11} Heel sts.

There should be 23{26-29} sts on first needle, 14{16-18} sts on second needle, 13{15-17} sts on third needle, and 24{27-30} sts on fourth needle for a total of 74{84-94} sts.

GUSSET DECREASES

Maintain established rib pattern across Instep.

Rnd 1: Knit across the first needle; work across the second and third needles; knit across the fourth needle.

Rnd 2 (Decrease rnd): Knit across to the last 3 sts on first needle, K2 tog, K1; work across the second and third needles; on fourth needle K1, SSK, knit across: 22{25-28} sts on first needle and 23{26-29} sts on fourth needle.

Rnds 3 thru 20{22-24}: Repeat Rnds 1 and 2, 9{10-11} times: 13{15-17} sts on first needle, 14{16-18} sts on second needle, 13{15-17} sts on third needle, and 14{16-18} sts on fourth needle for a total of 54{62-70} sts.

FOOT

Work even until Foot measures approximately $1^3/_4\{2-2^1/_4\}$"/4.5{5-5.5} cm less than desired finished foot length *(see Sizing, page 86)*.

TOE

Rnd 1: Knit across to the fourth needle; move beginning marker to the first st on fourth needle. This is now the beginning of the round.

Rnd 2: Knit around.

Rnd 3 (Decrease rnd): K1, SSK, knit across first needle; knit across second needle to last 3 sts, K2 tog, K1; on third needle K1, SSK, knit across; knit across fourth needle to last 3 sts, K2 tog, K1: 50{58-66} sts.

Rnds 4 thru 21{23-27}: Repeat Rnds 2 and 3, 9{10-12} times: 4{5-5} sts on first needle, 3{4-4} sts on second needle, 4{5-5} sts on third needle, 3{4-4} sts on fourth needle for a total of 14{18-18} sts.

Slip the stitches from the second needle onto the first needle. Slip the stitches from the fourth needle onto the third needle. There should be 7{9-9} sts on both needles.

Cut yarn leaving a 12" (30.5 cm) end. Thread tapestry needle with end and graft the remaining stitches together *(Figs. 14a & b, page 91)*.

Repeat for second Sock.

JENNY SOCKS

The Shadowbox Cuff and the Little Tents Cuff, page 46, are subtly textured. If desired, you can also make a pair of socks working the entire leg in the Slip Stitch Ridges pattern instead of the Shadowbox or Little Tents pattern on the Cuff. In that case, extend the initial K1, P1 ribbing to 1½" to 2" (4 cm to 5 cm).

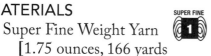 INTERMEDIATE

{ SHADOWBOX CUFF }

Finished Ankle Circumference:
7{8-9-10}"/18{20.5-23-25.5} cm

Size Note: Instructions are written for 7" circumference with 8", 9", and 10" circumferences in braces { }. Instructions will be easier to read if you circle all the numbers pertaining to your size. If only one number is given, it applies to all sizes.

MATERIALS
Super Fine Weight Yarn
  [1.75 ounces, 166 yards
  (50 grams, 152 meters) per skein]:
    2{2-3-3} skeins
  Note: If making the second size (8") with a total foot length longer than 9¾" (25 cm), a third skein of yarn will probably be needed.
Set of 5 double pointed needles,
  size 2 (2.75 mm) **or** size needed for gauge
Split-ring marker
Stitch holder
Tapestry needle

When instructed to **slip a stitch** (that is not part of an SSK decrease), slip as if to **purl** with yarn held to **wrong** side. (On **right** side rows or rnds, the yarn will be held at the **back** of work and on **wrong** side rows, the yarn will be held at the **front** of work.) This will prevent twisted stitches and also prevent the working yarn from showing on the right side.

GAUGE: In Slip Stitch Ridges Pattern,
        32 sts = 4" (10 cm)

Gauge Swatch: 4" (10 cm) square
Cast on 32 sts.
Row 1: Purl across.
Row 2: K2, slip 1, ★ K3, slip 1; repeat from ★ across to last st, K1.
Repeat Rows 1 and 2 for Slip Stitch Ridges pattern for 4" (10 cm).
Bind off all sts.

Instructions continue on page 44.

CUFF

Cast on 56{64-72-80} sts.

Divide sts onto 4 needles *(see Double Pointed Needles, page 88)*, placing 14{16-18-20} sts on each needle.

Place a split-ring marker around the first stitch to indicate the beginning of the round *(see Markers, page 88)*.

Rnds 1-6: ★ K1, P1; repeat from ★ around.

Rnd 7: Knit around.

Rnd 8: K2, slip 1, ★ K3, slip 1; repeat from ★ around to last st, K1.

Rnd 9: Knit around.

Rnd 10: P2, slip 1, ★ P3, slip 1; repeat from ★ around to last st, P1.

Rnds 11-34: Repeat Rnds 7-10 for Shadowbox pattern, 6 times.

LEG

Rnd 1: Knit around.

Rnd 2: K2, slip 1, ★ K3, slip 1; repeat from ★ around to last st, K1.

Repeat Rnds 1 and 2 for Slip Stitch Ridges pattern until Sock measures approximately 6³/4{7-7¹/4-7¹/2}"/ 17{18-18.5-19} cm from cast on edge **or** to desired length to top of heel, ending by working Rnd 1.

HEEL

Dividing Stitches: Work in pattern across first needle. Continuing with **same** needle, work across second needle, then K1 from third needle. Remove marker. The Heel Flap will be worked back and forth across these 29{33-37-41} sts.

Slip the remaining 27{31-35-39} sts onto a st holder for Instep to be worked later.

HEEL FLAP

Row 1: Purl across.

Row 2: Slip 1, ★ K1, slip 1; repeat from ★ across.

Rows 3 thru 26{30-34-38}: Repeat Rows 1 and 2, 12{14-16-18} times.

TURNING HEEL

Begin working short rows as follows:

Row 1: P 17{19-21-23}, P2 tog *(Fig. 12, page 91)*, P1, leave remaining 9{11-13-15} sts unworked; **turn**.

Row 2: Slip 1, K6, SSK *(Figs. 9a-c, page 90)*, K1, leave remaining 9{11-13-15} sts unworked; turn.

Row 3: Slip 1, P7, P2 tog, P1; turn.

Row 4: Slip 1, K8, SSK, K1; turn.

Row 5: Slip 1, P9, P2 tog, P1; turn.

Row 6: Slip 1, K 10, SSK, K1; turn.

Row 7: Slip 1, P 11, P2 tog, P1; turn.

Row 8: Slip 1, K 12, SSK, K1; turn.

Row 9: Slip 1, P 13, P2 tog, P1; turn.

Row 10: Slip 1, K 14, SSK, K1; turn.

FIRST SIZE (7") ONLY
Row 11: Slip 1, P 15, P2 tog; turn.

Row 12: Slip 1, K 15, SSK; do **not** turn: 17 sts.

SECOND SIZE (8") ONLY
Row 11: Slip 1, P 15, P2 tog, P1; turn.

Row 12: Slip 1, K 16, SSK, K1; turn.

Row 13: Slip 1, P 17, P2 tog; turn.

Row 14: Slip 1, K 17, SSK; do **not** turn: 19 sts.

THIRD SIZE (9") ONLY
Row 11: Slip 1, P 15, P2 tog, P1; turn.

Row 12: Slip 1, K 16, SSK, K1; turn.

Row 13: Slip 1, P 17, P2 tog, P1; turn.

Row 14: Slip 1, K 18, SSK, K1; turn.

Row 15: Slip 1, P 19, P2 tog; turn.

Row 16: Slip 1, K 19, SSK; do **not** turn: 21 sts.

FOURTH SIZE (10") ONLY
Row 11: Slip 1, P 15, P2 tog, P1; turn.

Row 12: Slip 1, K 16, SSK, K1; turn.

Row 13: Slip 1, P 17, P2 tog, P1; turn.

Row 14: Slip 1, K 18, SSK, K1; turn.

Row 15: Slip 1, P 19, P2 tog, P1; turn.

Row 16: Slip 1, K 20, SSK, K1; turn.

Row 17: Slip 1, P 21, P2 tog; turn.

Row 18: Slip 1, K 21, SSK; do **not** turn: 23 sts.

GUSSET
The remainder of the Sock is worked in rounds.

Slip the Instep sts from the st holder onto an empty needle.

FOUNDATION ROUND
With **right** side of Heel facing, continue with the working yarn and the needle that is holding the Heel sts and pick up 13{15-17-19} sts along the side of the Heel Flap and one st in the corner (where the Heel Flap meets the Instep) *(Fig. 13, page 91)*.

With an empty needle, work the first 13{15-17-19} Instep sts in established Slip Stitch Ridges pattern.

With an empty needle, work the remaining 14{16-18-20} Instep sts in pattern.

With an empty needle, pick up one st in the corner and 13{15-17-19} sts along the side of the Heel Flap, then knit the first 8{9-10-11} Heel sts; place a marker around the first st on the next needle to indicate the beginning of the round.

There should be 23{26-29-32} sts on first needle, 13{15-17-19} sts on second needle, 14{16-18-20} sts on third needle and 22{25-28-31} sts on fourth needle for a total of 72{82-92-102} sts.

GUSSET DECREASES
Rnd 1: Knit around.

Rnd 2 (Decrease rnd): Knit across to last 3 sts on first needle, K2 tog *(Fig. 7, page 89)*, K1; work in established pattern across second and third needles; on fourth needle K1, SSK, knit across: 22{25-28-31} sts on first needle and 21{24-27-30} sts on fourth needle.

Rnds 3 thru 16{18-20-22}: Repeat Rnds 1 and 2, 7{8-9-10} times: 15{17-19-21} sts on first needle and 14{16-18-20} sts on fourth needle.

Slip the last stitch on the first needle onto second needle. There should now be 14{16-18-20} sts on each needle, for a total of 56{64-72-80} sts.

Instructions continue on page 46.

FOOT

Work even until Foot measures approximately 2{2-2-2¼}"/5{5-5-5.5} cm less than desired finished foot length *(see Sizing, page 86)*.

TOE

Rnds 1-3: Knit around.

Rnd 4: Knit across to fourth needle; move beginning marker to first st on fourth needle. This is now the beginning of the round.

Rnd 5 (Decrease rnd): K1, SSK, knit across first needle; knit across second needle to last 3 sts, K2 tog, K1; on third needle K1, SSK, knit across; knit across fourth needle to last 3 sts, K2 tog, K1: 13{15-17-19} sts on each needle.

Rnd 6: Knit around.

Rnds 7 thru 18{20-22-26}: Repeat Rnds 5 and 6, 6{7-8-10} times: 7{8-9-9} sts on each needle for a total of 28{32-36-36} sts.

Rnds 19{21-23-27} thru 21{23-25-29}: Repeat Rnd 5, 3 times: 4{5-6-6} sts on each needle for a total of 16{20-24-24} sts.

Slip the sts from second needle onto first needle. Slip the sts from fourth needle onto third needle.

Cut yarn leaving a 12" (30.5 cm) end. Thread tapestry needle with end and graft the remaining stitches together *(Figs. 14a & b, page 91)*.

Repeat for second Sock.

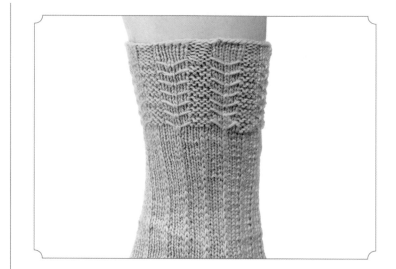

Finished Ankle Circumference:
7{8-9-10}"/18{20.5-23-25.5} cm

Size Note: Instructions are written for 7" circumference with 8", 9", and 10" circumferences in braces { }. Instructions will be easier to read if you circle all the numbers pertaining to your size. If only one number is given, it applies to all sizes.

MATERIALS

Super Fine Weight Yarn
[1.75 ounces, 231 yards
(50 grams, 211 meters) per skein]:
2{2-2-3} skeins
Set of 5 double pointed needles,
size 2 (2.75 mm) **or** size needed for gauge
Split-ring marker
Stitch holder
Tapestry needle

When instructed to **slip a stitch** (that is not part of an SSK decrease or the Little Tents pattern), slip as if to **purl** with yarn held to **wrong** side. (On **right** side rows or rnds, the yarn will be held at the **back** of work and on **wrong** side rows, the yarn will be held at the **front** of work.) This will prevent twisted stitches and also prevent the working yarn from showing on the right side.

GAUGE: In Slip Stitch Ridges Pattern,
32 sts = 4" (10 cm)

Gauge Swatch: 4" (10 cm) square
Cast on 32 sts.
Row 1: Purl across.
Row 2: K2, slip 1, ★ K3, slip 1; repeat from ★ across to last st, K1.
Repeat Rows 1 and 2 for Slip Stitch Ridges pattern for 4" (10 cm).
Bind off all sts.

CUFF
Cast on 56{64-72-80} sts.

Divide sts onto 4 needles as follows *(see Double Pointed Needles, page 88)*: 13{16-21-21} sts on first needle, 11{16-19-19} sts on second needle, 16{16-16-21} sts on third needle, and 16{16-16-19} sts on fourth needle.

Note: The distribution of sts ensures that when working Rnd 8, no "floats" have to go across a needle join.

Place a split-ring marker around the first stitch to indicate the beginning of the round *(see Markers, page 88)*.

When working the **Little Tents Pattern** on the **Cuff,** you will be instructed to slip 5 stitches holding the yarn in **front.** The strand forms a "float" on the right side, which will later be lifted up and worked under locking it in place and forming the pattern.

Rnds 1-7: ★ K5, P3; repeat from ★ around.

Rnd 8: ★ With yarn held in **front,** slip 5, K3; repeat from ★ around.

Rnd 9: ★ K5, P3; repeat from ★ around.

Rnd 10: K2, insert right needle tip under yarn float, knit the next st, pulling the new st under the yarn float before dropping the old st off left needle, ★ K7, insert right needle tip under yarn float, knit the next st, pulling the new st under the yarn float before dropping the old st off left needle; repeat from ★ around to last 5 sts, K5.

Rnd 11: ★ K5, P3; repeat from ★ around.

Rnds 12-34: Repeat Rnds 8-11, 5 times for Little Tents pattern; then repeat Rnds 8-10 once **more.**

LEG
Rearrange the sts so that there are 14{16-18-20} sts on each needle, taking care that the beginning of the round remains in the same place.

Rnd 1: Knit around.

Rnd 2: K2, slip 1, ★ K3, slip 1; repeat from ★ around to last st, K1.

Repeat Rnds 1 and 2 for Slip Stitch Ridges pattern until Sock measures approximately 6³/₄{7-7¹/₄-7¹/₂}"/ 17{18-18.5-19} cm from cast on edge **or** to desired length to top of heel, ending by working Rnd 1.

Beginning with Heel, complete same as Jenny Shadowbox Cuff, page 44.

Repeat for second Sock.

KRISTEN SOCKS

The stranded colorwork cuff uses only small amounts of the pattern colors – a great way to use up leftover odds and ends of yarn. Using medium weight yarn, these socks work up relatively quickly, and make great gifts. Choose from Diamond Cuff, Zigzag Cuff, page 52, and Net Cuff, page 53; or make all three pairs.

▰▰▰▰▱ INTERMEDIATE

{DIAMOND CUFF}

Finished Ankle Circumference:
7¹/₄{8-8³/₄}"/18.5{20.5-22} cm

Size Note: Instructions are written for 7¹/₄" circumference with 8" and 8³/₄" circumferences in braces { }. Instructions will be easier to read if you circle all the numbers pertaining to your size. If only one number is given, it applies to all sizes.

MATERIALS

Medium Weight Yarn
  [3.5 ounces, 208 yards
  (100 grams, 190 meters) per skein]:
    MC (Blue) - 1{1-2} skein(s)
    Color A (White) - 1 skein or approximately
      20 yards (18.5 meters)
    Color B (Red) - 1 skein or approximately
      20 yards (18.5 meters)
Set of 5 double pointed needles,
  size 7 (4.5 mm) **or** size needed for gauge
Split-ring marker
Stitch holder
Yarn needle

GAUGE: In Stockinette Stitch,
      20 sts and 26 rows = 4" (10 cm)

CUFF

With MC, cast on 36{40-44} sts.

Divide sts onto 4 needles *(see Double Pointed Needles, page 88)*, placing 9{10-11} sts on each needle.

Place a split-ring marker around the first stitch to indicate the beginning of the round *(see Markers, page 88)*.

Rnds 1-3: (K1, P1) around.

Rnd 4: Cut MC; with Color A, ★ K9{10-11}, M1 placing new st on same needle as last st made *(Figs. 6a & b, page 89)*; repeat from ★ around: 10{11-12} sts on each needle for a total of 40{44-48} sts.

Rnds 5-15: Knit around following Diamond Chart, page 50, Rows 1-11 *(see Fair Isle Knitting, page 92)*.

Instructions continue on page 50.

DIAMOND CHART

KEY

☐ - Color A
■ - Color B

Follow chart from right to left and from bottom to top.

Rnd 16: Cut Color B; with Color A, knit around; cut Color A.

Rnd 17: With MC, ★ K8{9-10}, K2 tog *(Fig. 7, page 89)*; repeat from ★ around: 9{10-11} sts on each needle for a total of 36{40-44} sts.

Rnds 18-20: (K1, P1) around.

LEG

Flip the needles upside down and rotate the Cuff stitches, so that the Sock is inside out with the purl side facing outwards. To prevent a hole at the beginning of the round, bring the working yarn to the back, slip the last stitch on the right needle onto the left needle, bring the yarn to the front and return the slipped stitch to the right needle; bring the yarn to the back.
Move the marker to the first stitch on left needle.

Knit every round until Leg measures approximately 4" (10 cm) from Cuff.

HEEL

Dividing Stitches: Remove marker. Using fourth needle, knit across first needle, K1 from second needle. The Heel Flap will be worked back and forth across these 19{21-23} sts.

Slip the remaining 17{19-21} sts onto a st holder for Instep to be worked later.

HEEL FLAP

When instructed to **slip a stitch** (that is not part of an SSK decrease), slip as if to **purl** with yarn held to **wrong** side. (On **right** side rows, the yarn will be held at the **back** of work and on **wrong** side rows, the yarn will be held at the **front** of work.) This will prevent twisted stitches and also prevent the working yarn from showing on the right side.

Row 1: Purl across.

Row 2: Slip 1, ★ K1, slip 1; repeat from ★ across.

Rows 3 thru 18{20-22}: Repeat Rows 1 and 2, 8{9-10} times.

TURNING HEEL
Begin working short rows as follows:

Row 1: P 12{13-14}, P2 tog *(Fig. 12, page 91)*, P1, leave remaining 4{5-6} sts unworked; **turn**.

Row 2: Slip 1, K6, SSK *(Figs. 9a-c, page 90)*, K1, leave remaining 4{5-6} sts unworked; turn.

Row 3: Slip 1, P7, P2 tog, P1; turn.

Row 4: Slip 1, K8, SSK, K1; turn.

Row 5: Slip 1, P9, P2 tog, P1; turn.

FIRST SIZE (7¼") ONLY
Row 6: Slip 1, K 10, SSK, K1; do **not** turn: 13 sts.

SECOND SIZE (8") ONLY
Row 6: Slip 1, K 10, SSK, K1; turn.

Row 7: Slip 1, P 11, P2 tog; turn.

Row 8: Slip 1, K 11, SSK; do **not** turn: 13 sts.

THIRD SIZE (8¾") ONLY
Row 6: Slip 1, K 10, SSK, K1; turn.

Row 7: Slip 1, P 11, P2 tog, P1; turn.

Row 8: Slip 1, K 12, SSK, K1; do **not** turn: 15 sts.

GUSSET

The remainder of the Sock is worked in rounds.

Slip the Instep sts from the st holder onto an empty needle.

FOUNDATION ROUND

With **right** side of Heel facing, continue with the working yarn and the needle that is holding the Heel sts and pick up 9{10-11} sts along the side of the Heel Flap *(Fig. 13, page 91)*.

With an empty needle, pick up one st in the corner (where the Heel Flap meets the Instep), knit the first 8{9-10} Instep sts.

With an empty needle, knit the remaining 9{10-11} Instep sts.

With an empty needle, pick up one st in the corner and 9{10-11} sts along the side of the Heel Flap, then knit the first 6{6-7} Heel sts; place marker around the first st on the next needle to indicate the beginning of the round.

There should be 16{17-19} sts on first needle, 9{10-11} sts on second and third needles, and 16{17-19} sts on fourth needle for a total of 50{54-60} sts.

GUSSET DECREASES

Rnd 1: Knit around.

Rnd 2 (Decrease rnd)**:** Knit across to last 3 sts on first needle, K2 tog, K1; knit across second and third needles; on fourth needle K1, SSK, knit across: 48{52-58} sts.

Rnds 3 thru 14{14-16}: Repeat Rnds 1 and 2, 6{6-7} times: 9{10-11} sts on each needle for a total of 36{40-44} sts.

FOOT

Knit every round until Foot measures approximately 1{1¹⁄₄-1¹⁄₂}"/2.5{3-4} cm less than desired finished foot length *(see Sizing, page 86)*.

TOE

SECOND SIZE (8") ONLY

Rnd 1: (K8, K2 tog) around: 36 sts.

Rnd 2: Knit around.

THIRD SIZE (8³⁄₄") ONLY

Rnd 1: (K9, K2 tog) around: 40 sts.

Rnd 2: Knit around.

Rnd 3: (K8, K2 tog) around: 36 sts.

Rnd 4: Knit around.

ALL SIZES

Rnd 1{3-5}: (K2, K2 tog) around: 27 sts.

Rnds 2{4-6} and 3{5-7}: Knit around.

Rnd 4{6-8}: (K1, K2 tog) around: 18 sts.

Rnd 5{7-9}: Knit around.

Rnd 6{8-10}: K2 tog around: 9 sts.

Rnd 7{9-11}: Knit around.

Cut yarn leaving a 6" (15 cm) end for sewing. Thread yarn needle with end and slip remaining sts onto yarn needle; gather tightly to close and secure end.

Repeat for second Sock.

{ ZIGZAG CUFF }

Finished Ankle Circumference:
7¼{8-8¾}"/18.5{20.5-22} cm

Size Note: Instructions are written for 7¼"
circumference with 8", and 8¾" circumferences in
braces { }. Instructions will be easier to read if you
circle all the numbers pertaining to your size. If only
one number is given, it applies to all sizes.

MATERIALS

Medium Weight Yarn
[3 ounces, 197 yards
(85 grams, 180 meters) per skein]:
MC (Lt Brown) - 1{1-2} skein(s)
Color A (Brown) - 1 skein or approximately
20 yards (18.5 meters)
Color B (Tan) - 1 skein or approximately
20 yards (18.5 meters)
Note: If making the second size (8") with a
total foot length longer than 9" (23 cm), a
second ball of MC will probably be needed.
Set of 5 double pointed needles,
size 7 (4.5 mm) **or** size needed for gauge
Split-ring marker
Stitch holder
Yarn needle

GAUGE: In Stockinette Stitch,
20 sts and 26 rows = 4" (10 cm)

CUFF

With MC, cast on 36{40-44} sts.

Divide sts onto 4 needles *(see Double Pointed
Needles, page 88)*, placing 9{10-11} sts on each
needle.

Place a split-ring marker around the first stitch to
indicate the beginning of the round *(see Markers,
page 88)*.

Rnds 1-3: (K1, P1) around.

Rnd 4: Cut MC; with Color A, ★ K9{10-11},
M1 placing new st on same needle as last st made
(Figs. 6a & b, page 89); repeat from ★ around:
10{11-12} sts on each needle for a total of
40{44-48} sts.

Rnds 5-15: Knit around following Zigzag Chart
Rows 1-11 *(see Fair Isle Knitting, page 92)*.

ZIGZAG CHART

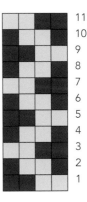

KEY

■ - Color A
□ - Color B

Follow chart from right to
left and from bottom to top.

Rnd 16: Cut Color B; with Color A, knit around;
cut Color A.

Rnd 17: With MC, ★ K8{9-10}, K2 tog *(Fig. 7,
page 89)*; repeat from ★ around: 9{10-11} sts on
each needle for a total of 36{40-44} sts.

Rnds 18-20: (K1, P1) around.

Beginning with Leg, complete same as Kristen
Diamond Cuff, page 50.

Repeat for second Sock.

{ NET CUFF }

Finished Ankle Circumference:
7¼{8-8¾}"/18.5{20.5-22} cm

Size Note: Instructions are written for 7¼"
circumference, with 8" and 8¾" circumferences in
braces { }. Instuctions will be easier to read if you
circle all the numbers pertaining to your size. If only
one number is given, it applies to all sizes.

MATERIALS
Medium Weight Yarn
[3 ounces, 197 yards
(85 grams, 180 meters) per skein]:
MC (Violet) - 1{2-2} skein(s)
CC (Green) - 1 skein or approximately
20 yards (18.5 meters)
Set of 5 double pointed needles,
size 7 (4.5 mm) **or** size needed for gauge
Split-ring marker
Stitch holder
Yarn needle

GAUGE: In Stockinette Stitch,
20 sts and 26 rows = 4" (10 cm)

CUFF
With MC, cast on 36{40-44} sts.

Divide sts onto 4 needles *(see Double Pointed
Needles, page 88)*, placing 9{10-11} sts on each
needle.

Place a split-ring marker around the first stitch to
indicate the beginning of the round *(see Markers,
page 88)*.

Rnds 1-3: (K1, P1) around.

Rnd 4: Drop MC; with CC, ★ K9{10-11},
M1 placing new st on same needle as last st made
(Figs. 6a & b, page 89); repeat from ★ around:
10{11-12} sts on each needle for a total of
40{44-48} sts.

Rnds 5-15: Knit around following Net Chart
Rows 1-11 *(see Fair Isle Knitting, page 92)*.

NET CHART

KEY
■ - MC
□ - CC

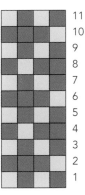

Follow chart from right to
left and from bottom to top.

Rnd 16: With CC, knit around; cut CC.

Rnd 17: With MC, ★ K8{9-10}, K2 tog *(Fig. 7,
page 89)*; repeat from ★ around: 9{10-11} sts on
each needle for a total of 36{40-44} sts.

Rnds 18-20: (K1, P1) around.

Beginning with Leg, complete same as Kristen
Diamond Cuff, page 50.

Repeat for second Sock.

LACY LEG WARMERS

Sizes	Finished Calf Circumference	Finished Leg Length
Small	8" (20.5 cm)	10" (25.5 cm)
Medium	10" (25.5 cm)	10½" (26.5 cm)
Large	12" (30.5 cm)	11" (28 cm)

Size Note: Instructions are written for size Small with sizes Medium and Large in braces { }. Instructions will be easier to read if you circle all the numbers pertaining to your size. If only one number is given, it applies to all sizes.
Choose a finished measurement that is 2" to 3" (5 cm to 7.5 cm) smaller than your actual calf measurement.

MATERIALS
Medium Weight Yarn
[3.5 ounces, 170 yards
(100 grams, 156 meters) per skein]:
1{1-2} skein(s)
Set of 4 double pointed needles,
size 9 (5.5 mm) **or** size needed for gauge
Split-ring marker

GAUGE: In Stockinette Stitch and in lace pattern, 16 sts and 22 rows = 4" (10 cm)

LEG
Cast on 32{40-48} sts.

Divide sts onto 3 needles as follows *(see Double Pointed Needles, page 88)*: 8{16-16} sts on first needle, 8{8-16} sts on second needle, and 16 sts on third needle.

Place a split-ring marker around the first stitch to indicate the beginning of the round *(see Markers, page 88)*.

Rnds 1-6: (K1, P1) around.

Rnd 7: Knit around.

Instructions contunue on page 56.

Rnd 8: ★ YO *(Fig. 5, page 89)*, [slip 1 as if to **knit**, K2 tog, PSSO *(Fig. 10, page 90)*], YO, K5; repeat from ★ around.

Rnd 9: Knit around.

Rnd 10: ★ YO, slip 1 as if to **knit**, K2 tog, PSSO, YO, K5; repeat from ★ around.

Rnd 11: Knit around.

Rnd 12: ★ K3, YO, SSK *(Figs. 9a-c, page 90)*, K1, K2 tog, YO; repeat from ★ around.

Rnd 13: Knit around.

Rnd 14: ★ YO, slip 1 as if to **knit**, K2 tog, PSSO, YO, K1; repeat from ★ around.

Rnd 15: Knit around.

Rnds 16-43: Repeat Rnds 8-15, 3 times; then repeat Rnds 8-11 once **more**.

Rnd 44 (Decrease rnd): ★ YO, slip 1 as if to **knit**, K2 tog, PSSO, YO, SSK, K1, K2 tog; repeat from ★ around: 24{30-36} sts.

Rnd 45: Knit around.

Rnd 46: ★ YO, slip 1 as if to **knit**, K2 tog, PSSO, YO, K3; repeat from ★ around.

Repeat Rnds 45 and 46 until Leg measures approximately 10{10½-11}"/25.5{26.5-28} cm from cast on edge or 2" (5 cm) less than desired finished length.

Work in K1, P1 ribbing for 2" (5 cm).

Bind off all sts loosely.

Repeat for second Leg Warmer.

SLIPPER SOCKS

Working without heel shaping has its advantages: it's relatively quick to work, easy for children to pull on without worry about heel placement, and ideal if you want to make a gift for someone whose exact foot length is unknown.

Shown on page 59.

■■□□ EASY

Sizes	Finished Circumference	Finished Length
Child	5¼" (13.5 cm)	10" (25.5 cm)
Pre-teen	6½" (16.5 cm)	11¼" (28.5 cm)
Adult Small	7¾" (19.5 cm)	13" (33 cm)
Adult Large	9" (23 cm)	15½" (39.5 cm)

Size Note: Instructions are written for a Child with sizes for a Pre-teen, Adult Small, and Adult Large in braces { }. Instructions will be easier to read if you circle all the numbers pertaining to your size. If only one number is given, it applies to all sizes.

MATERIALS
Medium Weight Yarn
[7 ounces, 364 yards
(198 grams, 333 meters) per skein]: 1 skein
Set of 4 double pointed needles,
  size 9 (5.5 mm) **or** size needed for gauge
Split-ring marker
Yarn needle

GAUGE: In Stockinette Stitch,
  16 sts and 22 rows = 4" (10 cm)
  In Spiral Pattern,
  16 sts and 26 rows = 4" (10 cm)

Gauge Swatch: 4" (10 cm) square
Cast on 16 sts.
Row 1: (K3, P2) 3 times, K1.
Row 2: P2, K2, (P3, K2) twice, P2.
Row 3: K1, (P2, K3) across.
Row 4: K1, (P3, K2) across.
Row 5: P1, (K3, P2) across.
Row 6: P1, (K2, P3) across.
Row 7: K2, P2, (K3, P2) twice, K2.
Row 8: (P3, K2) 3 times, P1.
Row 9: (P2, K3) 3 times, P1.
Row 10: (K2, P3) 3 times, K1.
Rows 11-26: Repeat Rows 1-10 once, then repeat Rows 1-6 once **more**.
Bind off all sts.

Instructions continue on page 58.

LEG

Cast on 21{26-31-36} sts.

Divide sts onto 3 needles as follows *(see Double Pointed Needles, page 88)*: 7{9-10-12} sts on first and second needles and 7{8-11-12} sts on third needle.

Because the number of stitches cast on is one more than a complete pattern repeat, a continuous spiral will form automatically as you work. It is not necessary to mark the beginning of a round or to keep track of which round you are on.

★ K3, P2; repeat from ★ working in continuous rounds until Slipper Sock measures approximately 9{10-11½-13½}"/23{25.5-29-34.5} cm from cast on edge.

TOE

Place a split-ring marker around the first stitch to indicate the beginning of the round *(see Markers, page 88)*.

ADULT LARGE SIZE ONLY
Rnd 1: (K7, K2 tog) 4 times *(Fig. 7, page 89)*: 32 sts.

Rnd 2: Knit around.

Rnd 3: (K6, K2 tog) 4 times: 28 sts.

Rnd 4: Knit around.

Rnd 5: (K5, K2 tog) 4 times: 24 sts.

Rnd 6: Knit around.

Rnd 7: (K4, K2 tog) 4 times: 20 sts.

Rnd 8: Knit around.

Rnd 9: (K3, K2 tog) 4 times: 16 sts.

Rnd 10: Knit around.

Rnd 11: K2 tog around: 8 sts.

ADULT MEDIUM SIZE ONLY
Rnd 1: K 13, K2 tog *(Fig. 7, page 89)*, (K6, K2 tog) twice: 28 sts.

Rnds 2-9: Work same as Adult Large, Rnds 4-11.

PRE-TEEN SIZE ONLY
Rnd 1: K 17, K2 tog *(Fig. 7, page 89)*, K5, K2 tog: 24 sts.

Rnds 2-7: Work same as Adult Large, Rnds 6-11.

CHILD SIZE ONLY
Rnd 1: K 19, K2 tog *(Fig. 7, page 89)*: 20 sts.

Rnds 2-5: Work same as Adult Large, Rnds 8-11.

ALL SIZES
Cut yarn leaving a 8" (20.5 cm) end for sewing. Thread yarn needle with end and slip remaining sts onto yarn needle; gather tightly to close and secure end.
Use yarn needle to weave in loose ends, weaving the cast on end into the outside of the slipper, so it will be hidden when the cuff is turned down. Turn down cuff.

Repeat for second Slipper Sock.

FOR BABY

When are socks the most fun to make? When they're knitted for tiny feet, of course! These three darling patterns start from the top and yield a ribbed cuff, a ripple cuff, or a lace edge at the ankle. All three designs can be made in three sizes, with two fitting 1 to 24 months and one fitting sizes 6 to 36 months. You'll want to make plenty of these to have on hand for baby showers!

RIBBED CUFF SOCKS

◼◼◼▢ INTERMEDIATE

Sizes	Finished Ankle Circumference	Finished Leg Length
1-3 months	4$\frac{1}{2}$" (11.5 cm)	4" (10 cm)
6-12 months	5" (12.5 cm)	4$\frac{1}{2}$" (11.5 cm)
18-24 months	5$\frac{1}{2}$" (14 cm)	5" (12.5 cm)

Size Note: Instructions are written for size 1-3 months with sizes 6-12 months and 18-24 months in braces { }. Instructions will be easier to read if you circle all the numbers pertaining to your size. If only one number is given, it applies to all sizes.

MATERIALS

Super Fine Weight Yarn
[3.5 ounces, 425 yards (100 grams, 388 meters) per skein]:
    1 skein
Set of 4 double pointed needles,
    size 2 (2.75 mm) **or** size needed for gauge
Split-ring marker
Stitch holder
Tapestry needle

GAUGE: In Stockinette Stitch,
32 sts and 44 rows = 4" (10 cm)

Instructions continue on page 64.

CUFF

Cast on 36{40-44} sts.

Divide sts onto 3 needles as follows *(see Double Pointed Needles, page 88)*: 12{16-16} sts on first needle, 12 sts on second needle, and 12{12-16} sts on third needle.

Place a split-ring marker around the first stitch to indicate the beginning of the round *(see Markers, page 88)*.

Work in K2, P2 ribbing for 3{3¼-3½}"/ 7.5{8.5-9} cm.

LEG

Knit 1{2-3} rnd(s).

HEEL

Dividing Stitches: Slip first 6{4-6} sts from second needle onto first needle. Remove marker. The Heel Flap will be worked back and forth across these 18{20-22} sts.

Slip the remaining 18{20-22} sts onto a st holder for Instep to be worked later.

HEEL FLAP

When instructed to **slip a stitch** (that is not part of an SSK decrease), slip as if to **purl** with yarn held to **wrong** side. (On **right** side rows, the yarn will be held at the **back** of work and on **wrong** side rows, the yarn will be held at the **front** of work.) This will prevent twisted stitches and also prevent the working yarn from showing on the right side.

Row 1: Slip 1, knit across.

Row 2: Slip 1, purl across.

Rows 3 thru 18{20-22}: Repeat Rows 1 and 2, 8{9-10} times.

TURNING HEEL

Begin working short rows as follows:

Row 1: Slip 1, K 10{11-12}, SSK *(Figs. 9a-c, page 90)*, K1, leave remaining 4{5-6} sts unworked; **turn**.

Row 2: Slip 1, P5, P2 tog *(Fig. 12, page 91)*, P1, leave remaining 4{5-6} sts unworked; turn.

Row 3: Slip 1, K6, SSK, K1; turn.

Row 4: Slip 1, P7, P2 tog, P1; turn.

Row 5: Slip 1, K8, SSK, K1; turn.

Row 6: Slip 1, P9, P2 tog, P1; turn.

SIZE 6-12 MONTHS ONLY
Row 7: Slip 1, K 10, SSK; turn.

Row 8: Slip 1, P 10, P2 tog; turn: 12 sts.

SIZE 18-24 MONTHS ONLY
Row 7: Slip 1, K 10, SSK, K1; turn.

Row 8: Slip 1, P 11, P2 tog, P1; turn: 14 sts.

GUSSET

The remainder of the Sock is worked in rounds.

Slip the Instep sts from the st holder onto an empty needle.

FOUNDATION ROUND

With **right** side of Heel facing, knit across, pick up 9{10-11} sts along the side of the Heel Flap and one st in the corner (where the Heel Flap meets the Instep) *(Fig. 13, page 91)*.

With an empty needle, knit 18{20-22} Instep sts.

With an empty needle, pick up one st in the corner and 9{10-11} sts along the side of the Heel Flap, then knit the first 6{6-7} Heel sts; place marker around the first st on the next needle to indicate the beginning of the round.

There should be 16{17-19} sts on first needle, 18{20-22} sts on second needle, and 16{17-19} sts on third needle for a total of 50{54-60} sts.

GUSSET DECREASES

Rnd 1 (Decrease rnd): Knit across to last 3 sts on first needle, K2 tog *(Fig. 7, page 89)*, K1; knit across second needle; on third needle K1, SSK, knit across: 15{16-18} sts on first and third needles.

Rnd 2: Knit around.

Rnds 3 thru 14{14-16}: Repeat Rnds 1 and 2, 6{6-7} times: 9{10-11} sts on first and third needles, and 18{20-22} sts on second needle for a total of 36{40-44} sts.

FOOT

Knit every round until Foot measures approximately 3{3¼-3¾}"/7.5{8.5-9.5} cm from the back of the Heel **or** 1{1-1¼}"/2.5{2.5-3} cm less than desired finished foot length.

TOE

Rnd 1 (Decrease rnd): Knit across to last 3 sts on first needle, K2 tog, K1; on second needle K1, SSK, knit across to last 3 sts, K2 tog, K1; on third needle K1, SSK, knit across: 32{36-40} sts.

Rnd 2: Knit around.

Rnds 3 thru 9{11-13}: Repeat Rnds 1 and 2, 3{4-5} times; then repeat Rnd 1 once **more**: 4 sts on first and third needles, and 8 sts on second needle for a total of 16 sts.

Using the third needle, knit across first needle. There should be 8 sts on both needles.

Cut yarn leaving a 8" (20.5 cm) end. Thread tapestry needle with end and graft the remaining stitches together *(Figs. 14a & b, page 91)*.

Repeat for second Sock.

LACE EDGE SOCKS

Sizes	Finished Ankle Circumference	Finished Leg Length
1-3 months	4$^1/_2$" (11.5 cm)	4" (10 cm)
6-12 months	5" (12.5 cm)	4$^1/_2$" (11.5 cm)
18-24 months	5$^1/_2$" (14 cm)	5" (12.5 cm)

Size Note: Instructions are written for size 1-3 months with sizes 6-12 months and 18-24 months in braces { }. Instructions will be easier to read if you circle all the numbers pertaining to your size. If only one number is given, it applies to all sizes.

MATERIALS

Super Fine Weight Yarn
[1.76 ounces, 213 yards
(50 grams, 195 meters) per skein]:
MC (Variegated) - 1 skein
CC (Cream) - 1 skein or approximately
20 yards (18.5 meters)
Set of 4 double pointed needles,
size 2 (2.75 mm) **or** size needed for gauge
Split-ring marker
Stitch holder
Tapestry needle

GAUGE: In Stockinette Stitch,
32 sts and 44 rows = 4" (10 cm)

Instructions continue on page 68.

When instructed to **slip a stitch** (that is not part of an SSK decrease), slip as if to **purl** with yarn held to **wrong** side. (On **right** side rows, the yarn will be held at the **back** of work and on **wrong** side rows, the yarn will be held at the **front** of work.) This will prevent twisted stitches and also prevent the working yarn from showing on the right side.

LACE EDGING
With CC, cast on 6 sts.

Row 1 (Right side): K5, P1.

Row 2: Slip 1, K1, YO *(Fig. 5, page 89)*, K2 tog *(Fig. 7, page 89)*, K1, YO, K1: 7 sts.

Row 3: K6, P1.

Row 4: Slip 1, K1, YO, K2 tog, K2, YO, K1: 8 sts.

Row 5: K7, P1.

Row 6: Slip 1, K1, YO, K2 tog, K1, YO, K2, YO, K1: 10 sts.

Row 7: K9, P1.

Row 8: Slip 1, K1, YO, K2 tog, K6.

Row 9: Bind off 4 sts, K4, P1: 6 sts.

Rows 10 thru 65{73-81}: Repeat Rows 2-9, 7{8-9} times.

There should be 32{36-40} slipped stitches along the straight side of the Edging.

Bind off all sts in **knit**.

LEG
With **wrong** side facing and using MC, pick up 32{36-40} sts along the straight edge of the Lace Edging *(Fig. 13, page 91)*.

Divide sts onto 3 needles as follows *(see Double Pointed Needles, page 88)*: 11{12-14} sts on first needle, 11{12-13} sts on second needle, and 10{12-13} sts on third needle.

Place a split-ring marker around the first stitch to indicate the beginning of the round *(see Markers, page 88)*.

Rnd 1: Knit around.

Rnd 2 (Increase rnd): ★ K8{9-10}, M1 *(Figs. 6a & b, page 89)*; repeat from ★ around: 12{13-15} sts on first needle, 12{13-14} sts on second needle, and 12{14-15} sts on third needle for a total of 36{40-44} sts.

Knit every round until Leg measures approximately 2{2^1/$_4$-2^3/$_4$}"/5{5.5-7} cm.

HEEL
Dividing Stitches: Slip first 6{7-7} sts from second needle onto first needle. Remove marker. The Heel Flap will be worked back and forth across these 18{20-22} sts.

Slip the remaining 18{20-22} sts onto a st holder for Instep to be worked later.

HEEL FLAP
Row 1: Slip 1, knit across.

Row 2: Slip 1, purl across.

Rows 3 thru 18{20-22}: Repeat Rows 1 and 2, 8{9-10} times.

TURNING HEEL
Begin working short rows as follows:

Row 1: Slip 1, K 10{11-12}, SSK *(Figs. 9a-c, page 90)*, K1, leave remaining 4{5-6} sts unworked; **turn**.

Row 2: Slip 1, P5, P2 tog *(Fig. 12, page 91)*, P1, leave remaining 4{5-6} sts unworked; turn.

Row 3: Slip 1, K6, SSK, K1; turn.

Row 4: Slip 1, P7, P2 tog, P1; turn.

Row 5: Slip 1, K8, SSK, K1; turn.

Row 6: Slip 1, P9, P2 tog, P1; turn.

SIZE 6-12 MONTHS ONLY
Row 7: Slip 1, K 10, SSK; turn.

Row 8: Slip 1, P 10, P2 tog; turn: 12 sts.

SIZE 18-24 MONTHS ONLY
Row 7: Slip 1, K 10, SSK, K1; turn.

Row 8: Slip 1, P 11, P2 tog, P1; turn: 14 sts.

GUSSET
The remainder of the Sock is worked in rounds.

Slip the Instep sts from the st holder onto an empty needle.

FOUNDATION ROUND
With **right** side of Heel facing, knit across, pick up 9{10-11} sts along the side of the Heel Flap and one st in the corner (where the Heel Flap meets the Instep).

With an empty needle, knit 18{20-22} Instep sts.

With an empty needle, pick up one st in the corner and 9{10-11} sts along the side of the Heel Flap, then knit the first 6{6-7} Heel sts; place marker around the first st on the next needle to indicate the beginning of the round.

There should be 16{17-19} sts on first needle, 18{20-22} sts on second needle, and 16{17-19} sts on third needle for a total of 50{54-60} sts.

GUSSET DECREASES
Rnd 1 (Decrease rnd)**:** Knit across to last 3 sts on first needle, K2 tog, K1; knit across second needle; on third needle K1, SSK, knit across: 15{16-18} sts on first and third needles.

Rnd 2: Knit around.

Rnds 3 thru 14{14-16}: Repeat Rnds 1 and 2, 6{6-7} times: 9{10-11} sts on first and third needles, and 18{20-22} sts on second needle for a total of 36{40-44} sts.

FOOT
Knit every round until Foot measures approximately 3{3$\frac{1}{4}$-3$\frac{3}{4}$}"/7.5{8.5-9.5} cm from the back of the Heel **or** 1{1-1$\frac{1}{4}$}"/2.5{2.5-3} cm less than desired finished foot length.

TOE
Rnd 1 (Decrease rnd)**:** Knit across to last 3 sts on first needle, K2 tog, K1; on second needle K1, SSK, knit across to last 3 sts, K2 tog, K1; on third needle K1, SSK, knit across: 32{36-40} sts.

Rnd 2: Knit around.

Rnds 3 thru 9{11-13}: Repeat Rnds 1 and 2, 3{4-5} times; then repeat Rnd 1 once **more**: 4 sts on first and third needles, and 8 sts on second needle for a total of 16 sts.

Using the third needle, knit across first needle. There should be 8 sts on both needles.

Cut yarn leaving an 8" (20.5 cm) end. Thread tapestry needle with end and graft the remaining stitches together *(Figs. 14a & b, page 91)*.

Sew the cast on and bound off edges of the Lace Edging together. Fold Edging to outside of Sock to form cuff.

Repeat for second Sock.

RIPPLE CUFF SOCKS

Sizes	Finished Ankle Circumference	Finished Leg Length
6-12 months	5" (12.5 cm)	4^1/$_2$" (11.5 cm)
18-24 months	5^1/$_2$" (14 cm)	5" (12.5 cm)
24-36 months	6^1/$_4$" (16 cm)	7" (18 cm)

Size Note: Instructions are written for size 6-12 months with sizes 18-24 months and 24-36 months in braces { }. Instructions will be easier to read if you circle all the numbers pertaining to your size. If only one number is given, it applies to all sizes.

MATERIALS

Super Fine Weight Yarn
[1.75 ounces, 166 yards
(50 grams, 152 meters) per skein]:
   MC (Ecru) - 1 skein
   CC (Variegated) - 1 skein or approximately
     20 yards (18.5 meters)
Set of 4 double pointed needles,
   size 3 (3.25 mm) **or** size needed for gauge
Split-ring marker
Stitch holder
Tapestry needle

GAUGE: In Stockinette Stitch,
   28 sts and 42 rows = 4" (10 cm)

Instructions continue on page 72.

CUFF

Using variegated yarn for the Contrasting Color really livens up a simple color pattern. To ensure that the two socks match, be sure to start the cast on for each at the same point in the yarn color repeat.

With CC, cast on 34{38-44} sts.

Divide sts onto 3 needles as follows *(see Double Pointed Needles, page 88)*: 11{13-15} sts on first and second needles, and 12{12-14} sts on third needle.

Place a split-ring marker around the first stitch to indicate the beginning of the round *(see Markers, page 88)*.

Rnd 1: Knit around.

Rnd 2: Purl around.

Rnds 3 thru 6{8-10}: Repeat Rnds 1 and 2, 2{3-4} times.

Rnd 7{9-11}: Knit around working M1 increase 2{4-4} times evenly spaced *(Figs. 6a & b, page 89)*: 36{42-48} sts.

Rnds 8{10-12} thru 16{18-20}: Knit around following Rows 1-9 of Ripple Chart *(see Fair Isle Knitting, page 92)*.

Cut CC.

RIPPLE CHART

KEY
☐ - MC
▧ - CC

Follow chart from right to left and from bottom to top.

LEG

Sizes 18-24 Months & 24-36 Months Only - Decrease Rnd: With MC, knit around decreasing {2-4} sts evenly spaced *(Fig. 7, page 89)*: {40-44} sts.

All Sizes: Rearrange the sts so there are 12{13-15} sts on first and second needles, and 12{14-14} sts on third needle, taking care that the beginning of the round remains in the same place.

With MC, knit every round until Sock measures approximately 2{2¼-2¾}"/5{5.5-7} cm from cast on edge.

HEEL

Dividing Stitches: Slip first 6{7-7} sts from second needle onto first needle. Remove marker. The Heel Flap will be worked back and forth across these 18{20-22} sts.

Slip the remaining 18{20-22} sts onto a st holder for Instep to be worked later.

HEEL FLAP

When instructed to **slip a stitch** (that is not part of an SSK decrease), slip as if to **purl** with yarn held to **wrong** side. (On **right** side rows, the yarn will be held at the **back** of work and on **wrong** side rows, the yarn will be held at the **front** of work.) This will prevent twisted stitches and also prevent the working yarn from showing on the right side.

Row 1: Slip 1, knit across.

Row 2: Slip 1, purl across.

Rows 3 thru 18{20-22}: Repeat Rows 1 and 2, 8{9-10} times.

TURNING HEEL
Begin working short rows as follows:

Row 1: Slip 1, K 10{11-12}, SSK *(Figs. 9a-c, page 90)*, K1, leave remaining 4{5-6} sts unworked; **turn**.

Row 2: Slip 1, P5, P2 tog *(Fig. 12, page 91)*, P1, leave remaining 4{5-6} sts unworked; turn.

Row 3: Slip 1, K6, SSK, K1; turn.

Row 4: Slip 1, P7, P2 tog, P1; turn.

Row 5: Slip 1, K8, SSK, K1; turn.

Row 6: Slip 1, P9, P2 tog, P1; turn.

SIZE 12-18 MONTHS ONLY
Row 7: Slip 1, K 10, SSK; turn.

Row 8: Slip 1, P 10, P2 tog; turn: 12 sts.

SIZE 24-36 MONTHS ONLY
Row 7: Slip 1, K 10, SSK, K1; turn.

Row 8: Slip 1, P 11, P2 tog, P1; turn: 14 sts.

GUSSET
The remainder of the Sock is worked in rounds.

Slip the Instep sts from the st holder onto an empty needle.

FOUNDATION ROUND
With **right** side of Heel facing, knit across, pick up 9{10-11} sts along the side of the Heel Flap and one st in the corner (where the Heel Flap meets the Instep) *(Fig. 13, page 91)*.

With an empty needle, knit 18{20-22} Instep sts.

With an empty needle, pick up one st in the corner and 9{10-11} sts along the side of the Heel Flap, then knit the first 6{6-7} Heel sts; place marker around the first st on the next needle to indicate the beginning of the round.

There should be 16{17-19} sts on first needle, 18{20-22} sts on second needle, and 16{17-19} sts on third needle for a total of 50{54-60} sts.

GUSSET DECREASES
Rnd 1 (Decrease rnd): Knit across to last 3 sts on first needle, K2 tog, K1; knit across second needle; on third needle, K1, SSK, knit across: 15{16-18} sts on first and third needles.

Rnd 2: Knit around.

Rnds 3 thru 14{14-16}: Repeat Rnds 1 and 2, 6{6-7} times: 9{10-11} sts on first and third needles, and 18{20-22} sts on second needle for a total of 36{40-44} sts.

FOOT
Knit every round until Foot measures approximately 3{3¼-3¾}"/7.5{8.5-9.5} cm from the back of the Heel **or** 1{1-1¼}"/2.5{2.5-3} cm less than desired finished foot length.

TOE
Rnd 1 (Decrease rnd): Knit across to last 3 sts on first needle, K2 tog, K1; on second needle K1, SSK, knit across to last 3 sts, K2 tog K1; on third needle K1, SSK, knit across: 32{36-40} sts.

Rnd 2: Knit around.

Rnds 3 thru 9{11-13}: Repeat Rnds 1 and 2, 3{4-5} times; then repeat Rnd 1 once **more**: 4 sts on first and third needles, and 8 sts on second needle for a total of 16 sts.

Using the third needle, knit across first needle. There should be 8 sts on both needles.

Cut yarn leaving a 8" (20.5 cm) end. Thread tapestry needle with end and graft the remaining stitches together *(Figs. 14a & b, page 91)*.

Repeat for second Sock.

FOR THE HOLIDAYS

Truth be told, every kind of sock is fun to make, even when no one you know can wear them! These two traditional stocking designs just happen to be among Santa's favorites, so don't be surprised if he fills them to overflowing with goodies—perhaps more sock yarn? Follow the easy Nordic chart to make Scandinavian-style stockings, or create a fireside gift-getter that's neatly trimmed in trees and snowflakes.

NORDIC STOCKING

Finished Size: 12³/₄" circumference x 20" long
(32.5 cm x 51 cm)

MATERIALS
Medium Weight Yarn
[3 ounces, 197 yards
(85 grams, 180 meters) per skein]:
  Red - 1 skein
  Green - 1 skein
  White - 1 skein or approximately 50 yards
    (46 meters)
Set of 5 double pointed needles,
  size 7 (4.5 mm) **or** size needed for gauge
Split-ring marker
Stitch holder
Tapestry needle

GAUGE: In Stockinette Stitch,
    20 sts and 26 rows = 4" (10 cm)

CUFF
With Green, cast on 64 sts.

Divide sts onto 4 needles *(see Double Pointed Needles, page 88)*, placing 16 sts on each needle.

Place a split-ring marker around the first stitch to indicate the beginning of the round *(see Markers, page 88)*.

Work in K2, P2 ribbing for 1¹/₂" (4 cm); cut Green.

Instructions continue on page 78.

LEG

Rnds 1-47: Knit each rnd, following Nordic Chart Rows 1-17 once *(see Fair Isle Knitting, page 92)*; then follow Rows 12-17, 5 times **more**.

Rnds 48-57: Knit each rnd, following Chart Rows 18-27.

NORDIC CHART

KEY

■ - Red
□ - White

Follow chart from right to left and from bottom to top.

HEEL

Dividing Stitches: With White, knit across 3 needles. Place the 16 sts from the second and third needles onto a st holder for Instep to be worked later.

Remove marker. The Heel will be worked back and forth across these 32 sts.

To wrap on a knit row: Bring the yarn to the front between the needles. Slip next st as if to **purl**. Bring the yarn to the back between the needles and slip the same st back onto the left needle.

To wrap on a purl row: Bring the yarn to the back between the needles. Slip next st as if to **purl**. Bring the yarn to the front between the needles and slip the same st back onto the left needle.

Begin working short rows as follows:

Row 1: Using one needle and Green, knit across both needles to last st, wrap last st; **turn**.

Row 2: P 30, wrap next st; turn.

Row 3: K 29, wrap next st; turn.

Row 4: P 28, wrap next st; turn.

Rows 5-18: Continue in same manner, working one less st before wrap.

Reverse short row shaping as follows:

Row 1: K 14, knit the wrap and st it wraps together, wrap next st; turn.

Row 2: P 15, purl the wrap and st it wraps together, wrap next st; turn.

Row 3: K 16, knit both wraps and st they wrap together, wrap next st; turn.

Row 4: P 17, purl both wraps and st they wrap together, wrap next st; turn.

Rows 5-16: Continue in same manner, working one more st before wrap.

Row 17: K 30, knit both wraps and st they wrap together; turn.

Row 18: P 31, purl both wraps and st they wrap together; turn.

Row 19: Cut Green; with White, K 16; place a marker around the next st to indicate the beginning of the round.

FOOT

The remainder of the Sock is worked in rounds.

Slip the first 16 Instep sts from the st holder onto an empty needle, and the remaining 16 sts onto a separate empty needle.

Rnds 1-29: Knit each rnd, following Nordic Chart Rows 1-17; then follow Chart Rows 12-17, 2 times **more**.

Rnds 30-39: Knit each rnd, following Chart Rows 18-27.

Cut Red and White.

TOE

Rnds 1 and 2: With Green, knit around.

Rnd 3: ★ K 14, K2 tog *(Fig. 7, page 89)*; repeat from ★ around: 60 sts.

Rnds 4 and 5: Knit around.

Rnd 6: K4, K2 tog, ★ K8, K2 tog; repeat from ★ around to last 4 sts, K4: 54 sts.

Rnds 7 and 8: Knit around.

Rnd 9: ★ K7, K2 tog; repeat from ★ around: 48 sts.

Rnd 10: Knit around.

Rnd 11: K3, K2 tog, ★ K6, K2 tog; repeat from ★ around to last 3 sts, K3: 42 sts.

Rnd 12: Knit around.

Rnd 13: ★ K5, K2 tog; repeat from ★ around: 36 sts.

Rnd 14: Knit around.

Rnd 15: K2, K2 tog, ★ K4, K2 tog; repeat from ★ around to last 2 sts, K2: 30 sts.

Rnd 16: Knit around.

Rnd 17: ★ K1, K2 tog; repeat from ★ around: 20 sts.

Rnd 18: Knit around.

Rnd 19: K2 tog around: 10 sts.

Cut yarn leaving a 8" (20.5 cm) end for sewing. Thread yarn needle with end and slip remaining sts onto yarn needle; gather tightly to close and secure end.

HANGING LOOP

With Green, cast on 24 sts.

Bind off all sts.

Fold the Loop in half and sew to the top inside of the Stocking.

TREES STOCKING

Finished Size: 14¹/₂" circumference x 19" long
(37 cm x 48.5 cm)

MATERIALS

Medium Weight Yarn
[3.5 ounces, 190 yards
(99 grams, 174 meters) per skein]:
Green - 1 skein
Red - 1 skein
White - 1 skein or approximately 30 yards
(27.5 meters)
16" (40.5 cm) Circular needle,
size 9 (5.5 mm) **or** size needed for gauge
Set of 5 double pointed needles,
size 9 (5.5 mm) **or** size needed for gauge
Split-ring marker
Stitch holder
Tapestry needle

GAUGE: In Stockinette Stitch,
16 sts and 22 rows = 4" (10 cm)

LEG

Using circular needle and Red, cast on 60 sts.

Place a split-ring marker around the first stitch to
indicate the beginning of the round *(see Markers,
page 88)*.

Rnds 1-12: Knit around; cut Red.

Rnds 13-38: Knit each rnd, following Chart,
page 82, Rows 1-26 *(see Fair Isle Knitting, page 92)*.

Instructions continued on page 82.

CHART

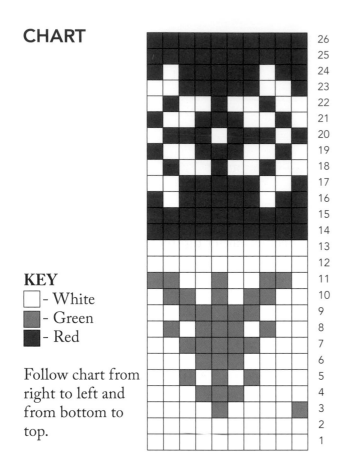

KEY
☐ - White
▨ - Green
■ - Red

Follow chart from right to left and from bottom to top.

Rnd 39: Cut Red and White; with Green, ★ K2 tog *(Fig. 7, page 89)*, K 28; repeat from ★ once **more**: 58 sts.

Knit every round until Leg measures approximately 11" (28 cm) from cast on edge, allowing edge to roll.

HEEL

Dividing Stitches: K 44; drop Green. The Heel will be worked back and forth leaving unworked sts on circular needle.

To wrap on a knit row: Bring the yarn to the front between the needles. Slip next st as if to **purl**. Bring the yarn to the back between the needles and slip the same st back onto the left needle.

To wrap on a purl row: Bring the yarn to the back between the needles. Slip next st as if to **purl**. Bring the yarn to the front between the needles and slip the same st back onto the left needle.

Begin working short rows as follows:

Row 1: With Red, K 28, wrap next st; **turn**.

Row 2: P 27, wrap next st; turn.

Row 3: K 26, wrap next st; turn.

Row 4: P 25, wrap next st; turn.

Rows 5-18: Continue in same manner, working one less st before wrap.

Reverse short row shaping as follows:

Row 1: K 11, knit the wrap and st it wraps together, wrap next st; turn.

Row 2: P 12, purl the wrap and st it wraps together, wrap next st; turn.

Row 3: K 13, knit both wraps and st they wrap together, wrap next st; turn.

Row 4: P 14, purl both wraps and st they wrap together, wrap next st; turn.

Rows 5-16: Continue in same manner, working one more st before wrap.

Row 17: K 27, knit both wraps and st they wrap together; turn.

Row 18: P 28, purl both wraps and st they wrap together; turn.

Row 19: Cut Red, with Green, K 14; place a marker around the next st to indicate the beginning of the round.

FOOT

Knit every round until Foot measures approximately 5" (12.5 cm) from Heel.

TOE

Rnds 1 and 2: With Red, knit around.

Rnd 3: ★ K 27, K2 tog; repeat from ★ once **more**: 56 sts.

Rnd 4: Knit around.

Divide sts onto 4 needles *(see Double Pointed Needles, page 88)*, placing 14 sts on each needle.

Rnd 5: ★ K6, K2 tog; repeat from ★ around: 49 sts.

Rnd 6: Knit around.

Rnd 7: ★ K5, K2 tog; repeat from ★ around: 42 sts.

Rnd 8: Knit around.

Rnd 9: ★ K4, K2 tog; repeat from ★ around: 35 sts.

Rnd 10: Knit around.

Rnd 11: ★ K3, K2 tog; repeat from ★ around: 28 sts.

Rnd 12: Knit around.

Rnd 13: ★ K2, K2 tog; repeat from ★ around: 21 sts.

Rnd 14: Knit around.

Rnd 15: ★ K1, K2 tog; repeat from ★ around: 14 sts.

Rnd 16: Knit around.

Rnd 17: K2 tog around: 7 sts.

Cut yarn leaving an 8" (20.5 cm) end for sewing. Thread yarn needle with end and slip remaining sts onto yarn needle; gather tightly to close and secure end.

HANGING I-CORD LOOP

Using double pointed needle and Red, cast on 3 sts.

Slide the sts to the opposite end of the needle. The first st you will knit is at the opposite end from the working yarn. Pull the working yarn across the back and knit across.

Now slide the work again, give the cord end a tug, pull the yarn across the back and knit across.

Add some tension when knitting the first st, so the working yarn is pulled tight, after each row.

Repeat this process until the cord is 6" (15 cm) long.

Bind off all sts.

Fold the Cord in half and sew to the top inside of the Stocking.

GENERAL INSTRUCTIONS

ABBREVIATIONS

CC	contrasting color
cm	centimeters
K	knit
MC	main color
M1	make one
mm	millimeters
P	purl
PSSO	pass slipped stitch over
P2SSO	pass 2 slipped stitches over
Rnd(s)	round(s)
SSK	slip, slip, knit
st(s)	stitch(es)
tbl	through back loop
tog	together
YO	yarn over

★ — work instructions following ★ as many **more** times as indicated in addition to the first time.

† to † — work all instructions from first † to second † as many times as specified.

( ) or [ ] — work enclosed instructions **as many** times as specified by the number immediately following **or** contains explanatory remarks.

colon (:) — the number given after a colon at the end of a row or round denotes the number of stitches you should have on that row or round.

work even — work without increasing or decreasing in the established pattern.

GAUGE

Exact gauge is essential for proper size. Before beginning your project, make a sample swatch in the yarn and needle specified in the individual instructions. After completing the swatch, measure it, counting your stitches and rows or rounds carefully. If your swatch is larger or smaller than specified, make another, changing needle size to get the correct gauge. **Keep trying until you find the size needle that will give you the specified gauge.** Your gauge swatch will be most accurate if it is worked in the round in the stitch pattern specified. Once you have started your actual sock, check the gauge again after you have worked a couple of inches.

KNIT TERMINOLOGY	
UNITED STATES	**INTERNATIONAL**
gauge =	tension
bind off =	cast off
yarn over (YO) =	yarn forward (yfwd) **or**
	yarn around needle (yrn)

Yarn Weight Symbol & Names	LACE 0	SUPER FINE 1	FINE 2	LIGHT 3	MEDIUM 4	BULKY 5	SUPER BULKY 6
Type of Yarns in Category	Fingering, size 10 crochet thread	Sock, Fingering, Baby	Sport, Baby	DK, Light Worsted	Worsted, Afghan, Aran	Chunky, Craft, Rug	Bulky, Roving
Knit Gauge Range* in Stockinette St to 4" (10 cm)	33-40** sts	27-32 sts	23-26 sts	21-24 sts	16-20 sts	12-15 sts	6-11 sts
Advised Needle Size Range	000-1	1 to 3	3 to 5	5 to 7	7 to 9	9 to 11	11 and larger

*GUIDELINES ONLY: The chart above reflects the most commonly used gauges and needle sizes for specific yarn categories.

** Lace weight yarns are usually knitted on larger needles to create lacy openwork patterns. Accordingly, a gauge range is difficult to determine. Always follow the gauge stated in your pattern.

■□□□ BEGINNER	Projects for first-time knitters using basic knit and purl stitches. Minimal shaping.
■■□□ EASY	Projects using basic stitches, repetitive stitch patterns, simple color changes, and simple shaping and finishing.
■■■□ INTERMEDIATE	Projects with a variety of stitches, such as basic cables and lace, simple intarsia, double-pointed needles and knitting in the round needle techniques, mid-level shaping and finishing.
■■■■ EXPERIENCED	Projects using advanced techniques and stitches, such as short rows, fair isle, more intricate intarsia, cables, lace patterns, and numerous color changes.

KNITTING NEEDLES															
U.S.	0	1	2	3	4	5	6	7	8	9	10	10½	11	13	15	17
U.K.	13	12	11	10	9	8	7	6	5	4	3	2	1	00	000	---
Metric - mm	2	2.25	2.75	3.25	3.5	3.75	4	4.5	5	5.5	6	6.5	8	9	10	12.75

SIZING

Most of these patterns give the option for more than one size. Choose the size to knit by your ankle circumference. Measure your ankle with a tape measure, pulling the tape snugly. Subtract ½" (1.5 cm), and pick the ankle size closest to this total (if the total falls exactly between two sizes, use the larger one). Socks stay up best when they fit snugly around the ankle, and a little "negative ease" is a helpful thing. Keep in mind that eyelet, lace and cable patterns have more widthwise stretch than color stranded patterns and many slip stitch patterns.

If you need to accommodate a wide calf, pick your size according the ankle measurement, but work the first 2 to 3" (5 to 7.5 cm) with needles a size larger than the needles you used to get gauge, switching to the smaller needles for the lower leg and foot.

The length of the Leg is from the top of the sock to the top of the Heel and can be adjusted.

To determine the **desired finished length** of the Foot, you can measure the foot you are knitting for or use the chart at right. When measuring the sock to determine where to start the Toe, be sure to lay it down flat on a smooth, hard surface. The length is measured from the back of the Heel (not the spot where the heel meets the gusset.) Subtract the measurement specified for the Toe from the total foot length. Work the Foot to this measurement.

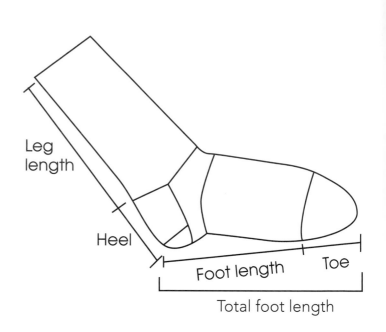

Woman's Shoe Size	Total Foot Length
5	8¾" (22 cm)
6	9" (23 cm)
7	9¼" (23.5 cm)
8	9¾" (25 cm)
9	10" (25.5 cm)
10	10¼" (26 cm)
11	10¾" (27.5 cm)
12	11" (28 cm)
13	11¼" (28.5 cm)

YARN SUBSTITUTION

Don't be afraid to try different yarns or color combinations. Most of the socks in this collection use Super Fine weight yarn, also commonly referred to as sock or fingering weight. The others use Medium (worsted) weight. In either case, a yarn in the same weight classification can be substituted for the yarns used in the sample models, as long as you can achieve a fabric that pleases you in the same gauge.

However, even within the same category, yarn thicknesses vary slightly. So when substituting, be sure to change needle size if necessary to achieve the pattern gauge, and examine the resulting fabric to make sure it is neither too loose and flimsy nor stiff as a board. For the best evaluation, wash and dry the swatch according to the directions on the yarn label. Two strands of a super light weight yarn held together can be substituted for a heavier yarn. Just be sure to make a swatch for gauge to see if the combination produces a fabric that pleases you. Also, keep in mind that yarns are put up in varying weights/yardages. If substituting, be sure to compare total yardage rather than the number of balls/skeins.

Consider the following factors as well:
Washability: Many people are happy to wash their hand knit socks by hand. If you are not one of them, make sure the yarn you choose is machine washable. This does not necessarily limit you to synthetic yarns, as many machine washable wool and wool blend yarns are now available. Check the washing instructions on the yarn label.

Breathability: Different fibers have different capacities to absorb moisture. Wool and cotton are very absorbent; acrylic and nylon are not. For some people, socks made of yarn containing a portion of natural fiber will be more comfortable to wear than 100% synthetic. For others, this is not an issue.

Elasticity: Socks need to "pull in" a little against the leg in order to stay up, so the yarn must have some ability to spring back to shape after being stretched. Wool and most synthetics have good elasticity. Alpaca and 100 % cotton do not. If you want to use these fibers, look for a blend that contains a relatively high percentage of a more elastic fiber.

REFINING THE FIT

It's a good idea to try on your socks "as you go". If your stitches are distributed on four needles, it is possible to pull the sock on, but there is a risk of dropping stitches off the ends of the needles. A safer method is to slip the stitches onto a length of waste yarn. Or slip them onto a 16" (40.5 cm) or longer circular needle.

If the socks fit at the ankle, you can make the following adjustments:
If the Cuff or Leg is too tight, make the leg shorter or cast on and work the first couple of inches using needles that are one size larger than needed to achieve gauge.

For a very narrow foot, work more decrease rounds in the gusset section. When you reach the toe, adjust the decreases as necessary.

For a very wide foot, work fewer decrease rounds in the gusset section. When you reach the toe, adjust the decreases as necessary.

If the socks are too tight across the instep, and the sock has a traditional "heel flap" heel, work a longer heel flap. For every two rows added, pick up an additional stitch along each side of the heel flap, and work an additional decrease round in the gusset section. (**Note:** this does not work easily on the "band heel," as there is no gusset section on that variation.)
For a sock with an "afterthought heel," as in the Elizabeth Fair Isle Socks, try working the heel on more stitches than specified in the pattern.

MAINTENANCE

Save some of your leftover yarn for repairs. If you see an area starting to wear thin, reinforce it by duplicate stitching (Swiss darning) over the worn area. This is easier to do if the sock is stretched slightly over a smooth hard surface. A darning egg is the classic choice, but a real egg (hard boiled) will do in a pinch, or even a rounded rock.

If holes develop in the toe, cut off the toe just below the hole and unravel the yarn back to the beginning of the toe decreases. Put the stitches back onto knitting needles and re-knit the toe with leftover yarn. If you don't have leftovers, try a coordinating or contrasting color (and think of it as a "design element").

Some people prefer to knit the heels and toes with a smaller needle for a slightly denser, harder wearing fabric. Others carry along a strand of reinforcing thread as they knit the heels and toes. "Wooly Nylon" thread is very suitable for this purpose. It is available at sewing supply stores and comes in a range of colors.

MARKERS

A split-ring marker is placed around the first stitch on the round to indicate the beginning of the round. Move it up at the end of each round.

As a convenience to you, we have used markers to help distinguish the beginning of a pattern, or to mark placement of decreases. Place markers as instructed. You may use purchased markers or tie a length of contrasting color yarn around the needle. When you reach a marker on each round, slip it from the left needle to the right needle; remove it when no longer needed.

DOUBLE POINTED NEEDLES

The stitches are divided evenly between three or four double pointed needles as specified in the individual pattern *(Fig. 3a)*. Form a triangle or a square with the needles *(Figs. 3b & c)*.

Do **not** twist the cast on ridge. With the working yarn coming from the stitch on the last needle and using the remaining needle, work across the stitches on the first needle.
You will now have an empty needle with which to work the stitches from the next needle. Work the first stitch of each needle firmly to prevent gaps. Continue working around without turning the work.

Fig. 3a

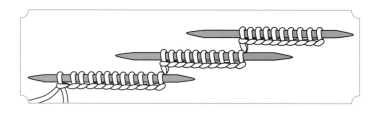

Fig. 3b

Fig. 3c

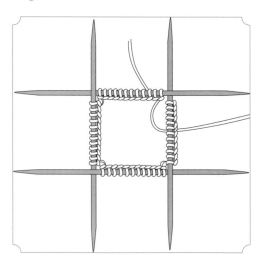

THROUGH BACK LOOP
(abbreviated tbl)

When instructed to knit or purl into the back loop of a stitch *(Fig. 4)*, the result will be twisted stitches.

Fig. 4

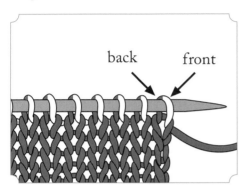

back   front

YARN OVER
(abbreviated YO)

Bring the yarn forward **between** the needles, then back **over** the top of the right hand needle, so that it is now in position to knit the next stitch *(Fig. 5)*.

Fig. 5

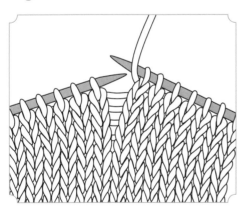

MAKE ONE INCREASE
(abbreviated M1)

Insert the **left** needle from the **front** under the horizontal strand between the stitches *(Fig. 6a)*. Then knit into the **back** of the strand *(Fig. 6b)*.

Fig. 6a

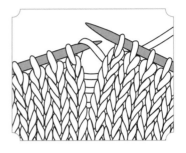

Fig. 6b

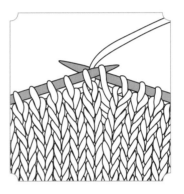

KNIT 2 TOGETHER
(abbreviated K2 tog)

Insert the right needle into the **front** of the first two stitches on the left needle as if to **knit** *(Fig. 7)*, then **knit** them together as if they were one stitch.

Fig. 7

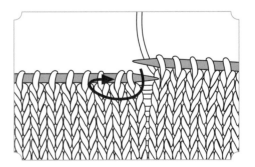

KNIT 2 TOGETHER THROUGH BACK LOOP
(abbreviated K2 tog tbl)

Insert the right needle into the **back** loop of the first two stitches on the left needle *(Fig. 8)*, then **knit** them together as if they were one stitch.

Fig. 8

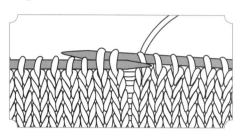

SLIP, SLIP, KNIT
(abbreviated SSK)

With yarn in back of work, separately slip two stitches as if to **knit** *(Fig. 9a)*. Insert the left needle into the **front** of both slipped stitches *(Fig. 9b)* and knit them together as if they were one stitch *(Fig. 9c)*.

Fig. 9a

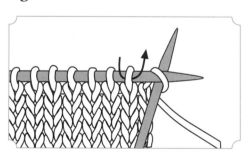

Fig. 9b

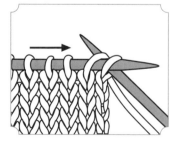

Fig. 9c

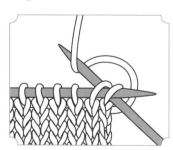

SLIP 1, KNIT 2 TOGETHER, PASS SLIPPED STITCH OVER
(abbreviated slip 1, K2 tog, PSSO)

Slip one stitch as if to **knit**, then knit the next two stitches together *(Fig. 7, page 89)*. With the left needle, bring the slipped stitch over the stitch just made and off the needle *(Fig. 10)*.

Fig. 10

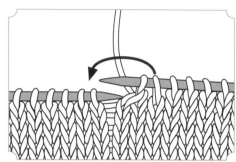

SLIP 2 TOGETHER, KNIT 1, PASS 2 SLIPPED STITCHES OVER
(abbreviated slip 2 together as if to knit, K1, P2SSO)

With yarn in back, insert the right needle into the front of the first two stitches on the left needle as if to **knit** *(Fig. 7, page 89)* and slip them off the left needle, then knit the next stitch. With the left needle, bring both slipped stitches over the knit stitch just made and off the needle *(Fig. 11)*.

Fig. 11

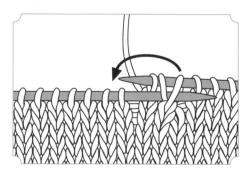

PURL 2 TOGETHER
(abbreviated P2 tog)

Insert the right needle into the **front** of the first two stitches on the left needle as if to **purl** *(Fig. 12)*, then **purl** them together as if they were one stitch.

Fig. 12

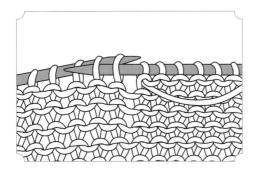

PICKING UP STITCHES

When instructed to pick up stitches, insert the needle from the **front** to the **back** under two strands at the edge of the worked piece *(Fig. 13)*. Put the yarn around the needle as if to **knit**, then bring the needle with the yarn back through the stitch to the right side, resulting in a stitch on the needle.

Repeat this along the edge, picking up the required number of stitches.

A crochet hook may be helpful to pull yarn through.

Fig. 13

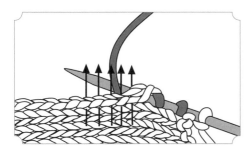

GRAFTING

Thread the yarn needle with the long end. Hold the threaded yarn needle on the right-hand side of work.

Work in the following sequence, pulling yarn through as if to knit or as if to purl with even tension and keeping yarn under points of needles to avoid tangling and extra loops.

Step 1: Purl first stitch on **front** needle, leave on *(Fig. 14a)*.
Step 2: Knit first stitch on **back** needle, leave on *(Fig. 14b)*.
Step 3: Knit first stitch on **front** needle, slip off.
Step 4: Purl next stitch on **front** needle, leave on.
Step 5: Purl first stitch on **back** needle, slip off.
Step 6: Knit next stitch on **back** needle, leave on.
Repeat Steps 3-6 across until all stitches are worked off the needles.

Fig. 14a

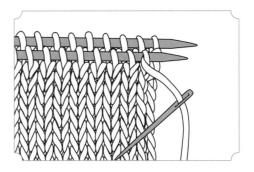

Fig. 14b

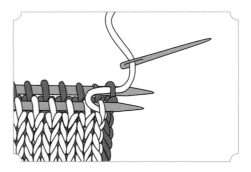

FAIR ISLE KNITTING

Fair Isle Knitting is a Stockinette Stitch technique that uses two colors across a row or round. Read all instructions and practice any techniques that are new to you before beginning your Sock.

WORKING WITH TWO COLORS

The two methods of knitting, English (holding the yarn with the right hand) and Continental (holding the yarn with the left hand), are easily combined when knitting in Fair Isle *(Fig. 15)*. It might be awkward at first, but it is faster than only using one method and allows the stitches to be uniform.

Fig. 15

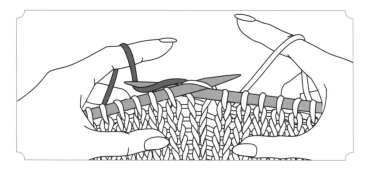

STRANDING

Stranding is the method in which the color not in use is carried across the wrong side of the fabric. It gives a nice appearance on the right side and also provides added warmth. Carry the yarn loosely across one to 4 sts, about 1" (2.5 cm) or less, without twisting the strands of yarn *(Fig. 16)*. Notice that each color is carried across the wrong side without crossing each other.

Fig. 16

When you use the English and the Continental method together, the strands automatically lie with the color that is held in your right hand on top. If one color is used more often than the other, always hold that color in the hand you usually knit with and the other color in the hand using the less familiar method. It is important to be consistent. If you only use one method of knitting, you must concentrate on always bringing one color from underneath and the other from the top.
Spread your stitches on the right hand needle as you knit so that you will have the correct tension on the yarn that is being carried. The stitches should be spread as much as the approximate gauge, so that the yarn carried will lie flat against the fabric. Carrying the strand slightly too loose is better than too tight, but be careful not to provide too much yarn as the stitches at end of the color section will enlarge. It's important to maintain the elasticity of the fabric.

CHECKING YOUR TENSION

The fabric should look smooth and even on the right side *(Fig. 17a)* without a puckered uneven appearance *(Fig. 17b)*. The strands on the wrong side should lie flat *(Fig. 17c)* without pulling the fabric or distorting the shape of the stitches *(Fig. 17d)*. If the strands are pulled too tight, the gauge will also be too tight making the Sock too small.

Fig. 17a

Fig. 17b

Fig. 17c

Fig. 17d

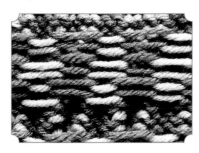

TWISTING STRANDS

If the strands are carried more than an inch, it can be difficult to keep tension. The strands can be easily snagged when putting the Sock on or pulling it off. To avoid carrying the yarn across 5 stitches, twist the carried color at its midpoint with the yarn in use. Make sure the carried yarn doesn't show on the right side or tighten the tension.

Drop the color you are using, lay the other color to your left on top of it, pick up the color you were using and continue working. The unused color is attached to the fabric *(Fig. 18)*.

Fig. 18

BOBBINS

Bobbins and yarn holders can be used to keep yarn manageable. Wind small amounts and refill as necessary.

FOLLOWING A CHART

Designs for Fair Isle knitting are worked from a chart. It is easier to follow a chart than written instructions and you can also see what the pattern looks like. The chart shows each stitch as a square indicating what color each stitch should be.

Visualize the chart as your fabric, beginning at the bottom edge.

Only one pattern repeat is given on the chart. This section is to be repeated around. Always follow the chart from right to left.

For ease in following the chart, place a ruler on the chart above the round being worked to help keep your place.

YARN INFORMATION

The socks in this leaflet were made using a variety of yarns. Any brand in the specified weight may be used. It is best to refer to the yardage/meters when determining how many balls or skeins to purchase. Remember, to arrive at the finished size, it is the GAUGE/TENSION that is important, not the brand of yarn.

For your convenience, listed below are the specific yarns used to create our photography models.

ELIZABETH SOCKS
Cascade Yarns Heritage
   MC - #5601 Black
Cascade Yarns Heritage Paints
   CC - #9824 Forest

STACY SOCKS Boxes & Dashes
Patons® Kroy Socks
   MC - #55042 Gentry Grey
   CC - #55008 Muslin

STACY SOCKS Vertical Stripes
Red Heart® Heart & Sole™
   MC - #3850 Navy Blue
   CC - #3935 Tequila Sunrise

ANNELISE KNEE SOCKS Crossed Cables
Lion Brand® Wool-Ease® Yarn
   #123 Seaspray

ANNELISE KNEE SOCKS Ladder Cables
Knit Picks® Swish Worsted™
   #24297 Allspice

EMMA LACE SOCKS
Lorna's Laces Shepherd Sock
   #Ons Natural

IRIS SOCKS
Cascade Yarns Heritage
   MC - #5604 Blue
   CC - #5602 Lt Blue

LUCY ANKLET SOCKS Zigzag Eyelet Cuff
Lion Brand® Sock-Ease™ Yarn
   #201 Rock Candy

LUCY ANKLET SOCKS Eyelet Rib Cuff
Knit Picks® Essential/Stroll Sock Yarn
   #23698 Burgundy

LUCY ANKLET SOCKS Little Fountains Cuff
Lorna's Laces Shepherd Sock
   #801 Sherbet

IVY SOCKS
Cascade Yarns Heritage
   MC - #5612 Green
   CC - #5618 White

JENNY SOCKS Shadowbox Cuff
Patons® Kroy Socks
   #55011 Flax

JENNY SOCKS Little Tents Cuff
Knit Picks® Essential/Stroll Sock Yarn™
   #24343 Granny Smith

KRISTEN SOCKS Diamond Cuff
Patons® Decor
   MC - #87643 Navy
   Color A - #87614 Winter White
   Color B - #87714 Barn Red

KRISTEN SOCKS Zigzag Cuff
Lion Brand® Wool-Ease® Yarn
   MC - #129 Cocoa
   Color A - #126 Chocolate Brown
   Color B - #403 Mushroom

KRISTEN SOCKS Net Cuff
Lion Brand® Wool-Ease® Yarn
   MC - #191 Violet
   CC - #172 Lemongrass

LACY LEG WARMERS
Lion Brand® Vanna's Choice® Yarn
   #151 Charcoal Grey

SLIPPER SOCKS
Red Heart® Super Saver®
   #0718 Shocking Pink

BABY SOCKS Ribbed Cuff
Bernat® Sox
   #42743 Hippi Hot

BABY SOCKS Lace Edge
Red Heart® Heart & Sole™
   MC - #3950 Watercolor Stripe
   CC - #3115 Ivory

BABY SOCKS Ripple Cuff
Patons® Kroy Socks
   MC - #55008 Muslin
   CC - #55605 Tutti Fruitti Jacquard

NORDIC STOCKING
Lion Brand® Wool-Ease® Yarn
   Red - #138 Cranberry
   White - #099 Fisherman
   Green - #174 Avocado

TREES STOCKING
Red Heart® Classic®
   Green - #0686 Paddy Green
   Red - #0914 Country Red
   White - #0003 Off White